Discovering Kwan Yin,
Buddhist Goddess of Compassion

Also by Sandy Boucher:

Opening the Lotus: A Woman's Guide to Buddhism

Turning the Wheel:
  American Women Creating the New Buddhism

Heartwomen: An Urban Feminist's Odyssey Home

The Notebooks of Leni Clare (Stories)

Assaults & Rituals (Stories)

Discovering Kwan Yin, Buddhist Goddess of Compassion

Sandy Boucher

Beacon Press
Boston

Beacon Press
25 Beacon Street
Boston, Massachusetts 02108-2892
www.beacon.org

Beacon Press books
are published under the auspices of
the Unitarian Universalist Association of Congregations.

04 03 02 01 00 99   8 7 6 5 4 3 2 1

This book is printed on recycled acid-free paper that contains
at least 20 percent postconsumer waste and meets the uncoated paper
ANSI/NISO specifications for permanence as revised in 1992.

Text design by Charles Nix
Text set in Rotis Serif
Composition by Wilsted & Taylor Publishing Services

Library of Congress Cataloging-in-Publication Data

Boucher, Sandy.
    Discovering Kwan Yin, Buddhist goddess of compassion /
Sandy Boucher.
        p.   cm.
    ISBN 0-8070-1340-4
    1. Avalokiteśvara (Buddhist deity)—Cult—United States.
    2. Women in Buddhism—United States.   I. Title.
    BQ4710.A84U623   1999
    294.3'42114—dc21   98-41118

For Crystal

Contents

One: Invitation

Rocks, willows, lotus pools, or running water are often indications of her presence. In the chime of bronze or jade, the sough of wind in the pines, the prattle and tinkle of streams, her voice is heard. The freshness of dew-spangled lotus leaves or the perfume of a single stick of fine incense recalls her fragrance.

John Blofeld, *Bodhisattva of Compassion*

As the feminine reasserts itself in Western spirituality, a towering female figure has arrived on our shores from Asia. Her name is Kwan Yin. She is the most revered goddess in all of Asia, and Chinese, Japanese, Korean, and Vietnamese immigrants naturally brought her with them when they came here. But her presence has also reached beyond the immigrant communities to enter the lives of countless European-Americans.

This small book explores the phenomenon of Kwan Yin's influence on women in the United States, and, true to the gentle goddess's simplicity and accessibility, it must open with the beginning of my own many-years-long relationship to her.

Kwan Yin first entered my life in the Midwest. This encounter was described in *Opening the Lotus*, but I want to evoke it here because of the many feelings associated with that event and because it situated Kwan Yin strongly in my consciousness. Like a random phrase of music that stays with a composer and develops over the years into a symphony, that first meeting with Kwan Yin began a rich association that called me to listen, learn, and stretch my understanding, and led eventually to the blending of themes that is this book. But most important is my desire that this music reach out and touch other people; I want to share my experience with the reader as an invitation to come closer to Kwan Yin and to our own compassionate natures.

The Kwan Yin I first saw presides over a room in the Nelson-Atkins Museum in Kansas City. She is a life-size wooden statue of a handsome and commanding woman. I was staying briefly at a communal household in Kansas City in 1982 when one of its inhabitants, who described herself as a Sufi (member of a Muslim mystical sect), invited me to accompany her to the museum to meet someone she called Kwan Yin. At that time I was active in feminist political work and had just written a book about women in the Midwest. I knew nothing about goddesses. But I was curious, and, particularly, I wondered why my new acquaintance thought that such a being as Kwan Yin might interest me.

The statue we went to see had been carved in wood in the eleventh or twelfth century in China. That is, it had come into existence about 800 years ago, in a time and a culture that were far beyond my comprehension. Yet this image communicated powerfully to me as I stood before her. Initially, it was her posture that struck me— a strong pose, in which she sits with one foot on the surface next to her, knee bent, with her arm resting casually on her knee. My Sufi guide told me this posture is known as "royal ease." What it conveyed to me was a self-assurance and relaxation, a grounded, loving, accepting presence that immediately intrigued me.

Then I was struck by the beauty of this life-sized image. Kwan Yin's clothing, in vibrant shades of scarlet, gold, and green, draped her body in graceful folds. It was caught here and there by a buckle, pulled tight by a knot; she wore an ornate necklace and bracelets, on her head rested a tall headdress. Her arms were rounded, her face even-featured, her body radiating health and vigor. She sat on a rock, one foot up, the other resting on a lotus blossom. All this drew me, as I admired the sensitive carving that had brought Kwan Yin out of the wood, the painting that decorated her in such splendid colors.

But most of all, as I stood in the museum room looking up at her, I felt the power of Kwan Yin's concentration and an inkling of the compassionate energy that my guide had told me she was supposed to embody. Her eyes looked downward, her face seemed utterly relaxed and inward-listening, her lips curved just slightly into a smile full of gentleness. In her posture and her face she held a stillness that I recognized from the rare moments in my life when everything fell into balance.

That image of strength, beauty, a radiant equanimity, and tenderness reached out to open a space in me wide enough to invite both my sorrow and my joy and awaken a sense of deep familiarity. Kwan Yin's face communicated the understanding of suffering; her presence demonstrated the magic of simply being here right now in this moment.

When I left Kansas City the next day, I took with me

a postcard reproduction of that statue and an awareness that something had been altered in me, some
human possibility suggested.

Later I discovered that her name means "She who
harkens to the cries of the world" and that she is believed to comfort human beings and save them from
disaster. She is the great Celestial Bodhisattva of Compassion in the Buddhist tradition (a "bodhisattva" is
a person who delays his or her full enlightenment in
order to aid in the liberation of all beings), but she tran-
scends Buddhism, being worshiped by people who may
know nothing of her Buddhist origin. Kwan Yin can be
confusing, for she manifests in numerous ways, and
the stories about her origins and her powers abound.
In the countries where she is honored, she has different
names: Guan Shih Yin in China, Kannon or Kanzeon
in Japan, Quan Am in Vietnam, Kwan Seum Bosal in
Korea. My use of the spelling Kwan Yin in this book is
chosen because it seems the easiest for Westerners to
pronounce.

I have taken up the task of writing a book about
Kwan Yin with great enthusiasm, hoping in this brief
volume to explore the origins of Kwan Yin in Asia, her
history and significance, and many of the stories that
enrich her legacy, and also to offer the reader some
practices with which to invoke her spirit. Readers whose
interest is piqued and who may want more detailed and
scholarly treatments can turn to the resources I have
gathered in the books and articles section.

To begin to know Kwan Yin, I had to delve into her
origins in China, and that led me to think about how
aspects of spirituality enter a culture. They come in

through people—individuals who recognize a particularly compelling expression of our humanity in a practice, a divine figure, a belief, a system, and make it real
in their lives. In just this way, Kwan Yin was incorpo-
rated into China many centuries ago. She started out in
Asia as a male figure, Avalokitesvara, bodhisattva of
compassion. Avalokitesvara was brought to China from
India in the fifth century C.E. For three hundred years
or so this bodhisattva was depicted as a male, albeit a
very androgynous one. Then in the late eighth century
a miraculous transformation occurred. Avalokitesvara
began to be perceived as a female and her name, translated into Chinese, became Guan Shih Yin. Although
there is no evidence of ancient matriarchy in China,
from earliest times female deities held sway in particular provinces. The Queen Mother of the West, who may
have originated with the Chou tribes of the western
provinces, is the most notable. Taoism also had a
mother figure, and unlike the earth mothers of other
ancient cultures, she was a celestial being whose all-
creative womb was the cosmos. The Divine Feminine
was never quite rooted out of Chinese culture by later
patriarchal religious and Confucian influences: it was
there to be resurrected in the figure of Kwan Yin.

Kwan Yin, or Guan Shih Yin, was first recognized in
the actual beings of supposed historical women, each
with her distinct personality and story. A typical story
would tell of a woman struggling against oppression,
who was mistreated, even killed, while sacrificing herself for the welfare of others. And then, after her death,
her abusers would realize that she had been not just an
ordinary woman but a goddess, Kwan Yin.

So in China Kwan Yin takes a number of forms, as

represented in stories and depicted in the multitude of paintings and sculptures of this goddess. Some of the better known manifestations include:

> The Thousand-Armed Kwan Yin
> Princess Miao Shan
> Kwan Yin of the South Sea
> White-Robed Kwan Yin
> Royal Ease Kwan Yin
> Water Moon Kwan Yin
> Mr. Ma's Wife
> Kwan Yin with Fish Basket
> The Woman of Yen-chou

We will meet these women/goddesses in the pages of this book and learn their stories. I have also included artworks depicting many of Kwan Yin's manifestations. The representations range in style and complexity from the very simple White-Robed Kwan Yin, often reproduced as a white porcelain statue, to the complex and esoteric Thousand-Armed Kwan Yin with its eleven heads, thousand arms, and forty-two ritual instruments understood only by initiates (see figure 1).

Scholar Chün-fang Yü summarized and explained the process of Kwan Yin's transformation for me when she wrote, "The original universal bodhisattva Avalokitesvara had to fit the mold of Chinese religious sensibility by taking on Chinese identities before Kuan Yin could succeed as the most popular Buddhist 'deity' in China." So this spirit or energy of Avalokitesvara/Kwan Yin entered the culture through the experience of flesh-and-blood people, in the forms that would correspond to their needs.

Figure 1. Thousand-Armed Guan Shih Yin on the altar at
City of Ten Thousand Buddhas in Talmage, California.
(Photo by Alan Nicholson.)

Looking at how Kwan Yin has come to America, I realize that she is making her way in the lives of today's women, too. Women call upon her for help, revere her, write poems or songs about her, embody her in her pure compassionate energy. Those of both European and Asian descent respond to her wide, tender mercy.

On a return trip to the Midwest some years ago I found a particularly arresting Kwan Yin statue. At the Ohio State Fair, in an exhibition hall sponsored by China, I saw a tall, green-painted Kwan Yin standing on a dragon, holding a graceful vase. Attached to the base of this statue was an ocean wave and balanced on its crest, a plump baby gazing up at Kwan Yin. It seemed that Kwan Yin was pouring the sacred fluid of life from her vial in a stream down to the child, whom I presumed to be the buddha. It was high kitsch and yet beautiful. Of course, I had to buy this Kwan Yin and bring her back to California, where I gave her to my friend Annie Hershey, a filmmaker and video artist, whose considerable gift for whimsy would allow her to appreciate it. Then in the mid-eighties my partner and I determined to create something that would introduce Kwan Yin to our own community and culture. We designed greeting cards carrying Kwan Yin's image; and the response from women who found the cards beautiful and inspiring convinced us that bringing Kwan Yin's image into the world was a useful endeavor.

Over the years I read what I could find on Kwan Yin, kept her image near when I meditated, and developed a guided meditation for the "Writing as Spiritual Journey" classes I teach, to help the students visualize Kwan

Yin and open to her. In my classes I discovered the difficulty many women have in giving compassionate
energy to ourselves, and I found that Kwan Yin can
help us do that.

But initially, I did not come easily to the idea of "goddesses." After all, I was a rational, politically active person who believed in the struggle for social change and
avoided any religious contamination. The last thing I
needed was a divine figure, of either gender, to show
me the way. But gradually over the years, as the energy
of Kwan Yin began to become real in my life, I had to
give up my skepticism and begin to articulate for
myself what the female sacred manifestations might
actually be. Now, for me, a "goddess" is several things.
First, an embodiment of human qualities, writ large.
So Kwan Yin represents compassion, love, hope, transformation, service—and the significance of her presence
in the lives of American women is that we are cultivating these capacities in ourselves. She is a spirit who
manifests in various forms to come to the aid of human
beings. She is the quintessential bodhisattva, the Buddhist practitioner committed to helping others. She
bears some resemblance to the Virgin Mary in the Christian tradition, and Jewish readers will recognize her
in their own Shekinah or "goddess full of mercy."
Whether Kwan Yin exists as an independent entity in
the universe or whether she exists in our minds and
hearts is not a question this book will attempt to
answer. I am open to both interpretations, and, as you
will see, the women in this book envision her in various
ways, depending on their circumstances. That is as it
should be, for Kwan Yin manifests in the form that will

be recognized, to each person differently. And ultimately, as some of the women in this book point out, to contact Kwan Yin is to be in deep communication with oneself.

In one of my classes, several years ago, a woman asked a fateful question: "Why isn't there a book about Kwan Yin written by a woman?" Once the question was voiced, I understood that such a book was needed, especially one that would explore Kwan Yin's impact on contemporary women's lives. I did not know if I would be the one to write it, but—just as we had put together the greeting card that would make Kwan Yin visible, understanding that somehow Kwan Yin had chosen us to do her work—I began to research and ponder this great goddess, thinking how I might write about her.

Then in 1995, two events brought me closer to Kwan Yin. On my way to the United Nations Fourth World Conference on Women in Beijing, I went to Pu To Island, the tiny dot of land in the South China Sea near Shanghai that is the home of Kwan Yin. Phyllis Pay, a Chinese-American friend who is a psychic and very interested in Kwan Yin, stayed with me on the island for six days. We both experienced Kwan Yin's presence strongly. A few months after returning from China, I was diagnosed with colon cancer, underwent surgery and six months of chemotherapy, and found myself talking to Kwan Yin. I received no answering visitations, but she responded, in a way, evoking a sense within me of balance and willingness to endure what I must.

Kwan Yin is even more present with me now that I am well, for I am meeting some profound psychological/spiritual challenges that send me for refuge into her broad compassionate energy. As a child I developed a way of being that mirrored my father's behavior. I am sometimes arrogant, critical, judgmental, impatient: often it is in my private life, with my partner, that I indulge these traits. Having come through the disastrous year of illness and loss, I now understand the hurtfulness of these tendencies in my life. These last two years have let me see that in my relationships I want to put aside these behaviors and act instead from a deeper impulse.

I am experiencing and cultivating an opening of my heart that allows for tenderness, for forgiveness, for a deep listening to others and myself. Kwan Yin has been part of this opening. Her spirit and her example help me to stay focused close to home and enable me to be intimate with my true nature instead of backing away into rejection or criticism. While sometimes I feel extremely vulnerable, Kwan Yin lets me realize that my only safety lies in the emergence of the tenderest part of myself, to meet the needs of each moment.

Over the years I have encountered more and more evidence of the presence of Kwan Yin—a statue in a masseuse's workroom, a picture on a book cover or conference brochure, a replica in a garden among the ferns and flowers, an altar to her in a Vietnamese restaurant, and another in the home of a friend. As I learned more about her, my interest grew (and I have described the evolution of my relationship to goddesses in general), but as I am a Buddhist, my devotion to Kwan Yin carries an inherent contradiction.

One evening, I gave a talk on Buddhism and spoke about Kwan Yin. A woman in the audience held up her hand and asked, "How is it that you have said you were drawn to Buddhism because it has no god, and yet you talk about a Buddhist goddess, Kwan Yin? I don't get it!" Of course, it was only a matter of time before somebody asked this very good and reasonable question. I answer it here—first, in case any reader may be wondering the same thing, and second, because I want to call attention to the several different significances of Kwan Yin.

It is true that one of the reasons I was comfortable in Buddhist environs as a feminist was the absence of an overweening father figure of a God. An important dimension of the Buddha is that he was a human being who achieved enlightenment, died, and completely disappeared. Original Buddhism, 2,500 years ago, took hold in India, in some sense, as a reaction against the prevailing Brahmanic religion, which included a pantheon of gods and goddesses. This earliest Buddhism (which we now call Theravada Buddhism and which exists in its traditional form principally in Southeast Asia) emphasized that one achieved enlightenment through one's own efforts, without the help of a divine intercessor.

Then, about five hundred years after the Buddha's death, a schism occurred between competing sects, or "schools," of the Buddha's followers, and Mahayana Buddhism was created. This form of Buddhism now includes Tibetan Buddhism, Zen, Pure Land Buddhism, and many other forms, and these traditions as they developed in several Asian countries took on cultural

and religious manifestations generally avoided in original Buddhism. Vestiges of earlier belief systems sometimes found their way into Buddhism and merged with
Buddhist beliefs and practices. Some of the Mahayana
traditions began to set up sacred emanations of their
own, dress them in gorgeous royal garments, and
revere them. Maybe people need their gods and goddesses. Certainly, people who worshiped indigenous
deities during the centuries before Buddhism might be
persuaded to convert if they were to recognize a powerful nature goddess in the guise of a Buddhist sacred
entity.

In my own Buddhist practice I am able to accommo-
date a fairly strict Theravada meditation and conceptual framework with an awareness of the "goddess"-
energy of Kwan Yin. That is, sometimes I do the very
spare insight meditation practice of watching one's sen-
sations and thoughts, avoiding the lure of particular
content; and sometimes I do meditations in which I
visualize the figure of Kwan Yin and invoke her
qualities.

But I understand that to use the term *god* or *goddess*
when speaking of a Buddhist sacred entity is to sim-
plify and obscure its true nature. In Asia, in particular,
there is a difference between the laypeople's perception
of such a figure and the view of it taken by a Buddhist
monk or nun. To an Asian peasant woman, Kwan Yin is
a powerful goddess, a divine being who cares especially
about women's concerns. She will come if you call her,
chant her name, put offerings on her altar. She will save
you from disaster, give you a child, heal your illness,
and lessen your sorrow. She is friend and mother, who

teaches compassion and patience in the crucible of daily life. She is as real as the wind in the trees. On the other hand, a Buddhist nun, chanting the same *"Namo Guan Shih Yin Pu-sa"* as the peasant woman, looks to the figure of Kwan Yin to help transform herself; she seeks through chanting and bowing and visualizing Kwan Yin to pass through into the spaciousness of true realization. That is, she views Kwan Yin as an aid to her practice, a symbolic figure whose compassionate actions teach and purify and ultimately show the way to liberation from suffering.

So we get an inkling of the complexity of this figure as she exists in the world, always interacting with people; Kwan Yin is *engaged* in the world; she manifests in many forms; she is revered and "used" in many ways by millions of people. The Asian mind may allow for more permeability of forms than our Western categorical thinking affords us. A sincere devotee of Kwan Yin may approach her in many ways, from the simplest petition for good health or help with a problem, to the most refined and subtle meditative experiences based upon practices involving Kwan Yin, and everything in between.

We approach Kwan Yin as who we are. We welcome her into our real, everyday lives. We open ourselves to her as our individual minds and hearts can understand her. This is how it has always been with Kwan Yin. She offers her myriad forms to us and promises only as much as we are open to receive in and from ourselves. She enters and becomes us, we enter and become her.

I invite you to come with me into the lives of women who know Kwan Yin. Chapter Two: "A Thousand

Hands" explores the world of Asian-American women, some of them in formal Buddhist monastic situations, as they experience Kwan Yin. In Chapter Three: "She Carries Me," we hear the stories of European-American women who live (with one exception) in contemporary secular settings. The majority of these women are from the West Coast, but they represent the many women in the Midwest, the East Coast, and other regions who have found Kwan Yin and made her part of their lives. Chapter Four offers ways to approach Kwan Yin: "Meditations, Songs, and Practices." Some of the many artistic representations of Kwan Yin appear throughout the book. And finally, there is a list for further reading in "Books and Articles."

May this volume open you to the beautiful, shining figure of Kwan Yin, and may she accompany you throughout your life.

Two: A Thousand Hands

If those who hold the name of Guan Shi Yin Bodhisattva
should fall into a great fire, the fire will not burn them,
because of Guan Shi Yin Bodhisattva's awesome spiritual
power. If they are tossed about in deep and treacherous
waters and call Her name, they will quickly reach the
shallows.

Wondrous Dharma Lotus Flower Sutra

Many women coming from Asia to live in the United
States bring with them stories of Kwan Yin. They
learned to revere her as little children, taught by their
mothers or grandmothers at the family altar, encour-
aged to offer flowers and fruit and incense to this powerful goddess. Particularly in the case of Vietnamese
women, Kwan Yin may have interceded in their
attempts to flee their country. In the refugee camps in
Thailand, where the Vietnamese found safety, large statues of Kwan Yin were constructed, for the Vietnamese
credit Kwan Yin with saving their lives and aiding their
escape. The boat people called on Kwan Yin, and many
believe that she saved their particular craft from the
storms, starvation, and pirates that brought other boats
to ruin. But Chinese, Japanese, and even Burmese
women also have experienced Kwan Yin as a compas-

sionate companion, an influence that continues in their new American lives.

Some of the Asian women I spoke to have become *bhikshunis,* or nuns, in the Chinese tradition of Buddhism and live what is still a very Asian lifestyle here in their adopted country. Other Asian-Americans are laywomen who participate fully in North American culture, who practice and teach Buddhism and work politically to create a more humane, safer world. Among these last, Kwan Yin is viewed with some ambivalence, for her influence on the expectations for women in Asian culture can be inhibiting for modern women. Despite some misgivings, Asian-American women still grant Kwan Yin a powerful place in their lives.

Kwan Yin in Men's Clothes

Kwan Yin had a striking genesis in Vietnam. Her story was told to me by a Vietnamese woman who lives in the northwestern United States with her American husband. Luong (not her real name) is a translator who has worked on a book project about the human losses of the Vietnam War. Her own first husband was killed in that war, and she translates the stories of other Vietnamese women whose husbands perished in the conflict. I am using a pseudonym because her family lives in Vietnam, and given the political situation there, she is cautious about any kind of public statement.

Luong's mother told her about Kwan Yin, or Quan Am, as she is known in Vietnam, when she was a little girl. Luong became fascinated by the statue of Kwan

Yin that stood in their home, and as she grew up, she learned that Kwan Yin represented strength and courage and patience.

She also learned the dramatic story of Thi Kinh, a real young woman who lived in ancient times, revealed to be Kwan Yin after her death.

The Trial and Transformation of Thi Kinh

Thi Kinh lived in a village with her parents. Her father, a farmer, owed money to his landlord and was unable to pay. As he could not make good his debt to this rich family, Thi Kinh's father offered his daughter in marriage to their son. The family did not particularly like Thi Kinh, but they took her because she was all they could get. Thi Kinh did not love the young man, but, as Luong says, "in the old days marriage was arranged by the families, and so you were expected to learn to love the husband as time went on." Thi Kinh married the young man, and they lived together, but, to his disappointment, she did not become pregnant and produce a child.

The husband had a mole on his cheek with a hair growing in it. One day as Thi Kinh was sitting sewing, she looked over to her husband, who was napping on the couch, and saw the hair in his mole. She was holding scissors, so she reached over to cut off the hair. Just then her husband woke up, and, startled, he accused her of trying to kill him with the scissors. Probably he only told that story to get rid of her because she had not produced a son for him. If she had tried to kill him, she would be sent away, and he could marry someone else.

The rich family threw Thi Kinh out of the house. The neighbors all gossiped that she had tried to kill her husband, and they would not help her. Her own parents did not want to take her back because they believed her guilty of such a crime. "For thousands of years," says Luong, "if a woman was thrown out of her family, what was she to do? Who was going to take her in? How was she to survive?"

Desperate, with no help from any direction, Thi Kinh hit upon an idea to save herself. She dressed in the robes of a monk and shaved off her long hair so that she looked like a man. Then she went to the Buddha temple and asked if she could stay there. She was accepted in the temple as a man, as a monk, and she began to work there and practice Buddhist meditation.

Unfortunately, one of the girls in the village who often saw the monk passing thought "he" was handsome and she developed a crush on "him." The girl, whose father was an important man in the village, longed for Thi Kinh, not knowing she was a woman. One night the girl heard a man passing her house and thought it was the monk; she invited him in and they had sex. When the girl became pregnant, her father was enraged. He beat her so that she would tell him who had fathered her child, and she did not know what to do. She told her father that the monk at the Buddha temple had made her pregnant.

When the people of the village heard this, they set out to punish Thi Kinh. She was thrown out of the temple and was once again homeless. "And in the meantime," Luong explains, "she remained silent. She did not say, 'I am a female, I cannot make her pregnant'; she said nothing. Now if she were to say, 'I am a female, I'm a woman,' then she would bring shame and embarrassment to this girl and her father. It would get her off the hook, but she had promised to Buddha that she would take to heart the Buddhist teaching to forgive and be patient and find peace. So she could not do this to this girl or her father." Silent, Thi Kinh endured the abuse of the whole community.

When the girl gave birth to her baby, the family gave it to Thi Kinh to raise. Now Thi Kinh faced another difficulty: How was she, a homeless monk, to care for a newborn baby? She set out with the child, going from village to village to beg for milk. The people were outraged at the shame Thi Kinh had supposedly brought on the name of Buddhism, in getting a girl pregnant. They threw mud at her, they threw rotten fruit and rocks at her.

Thi Kinh remained steadfast; she did not flinch before the abuse or renege on her vow of silence but went on trying to care for the baby. Finally, in a particularly vicious attack Thi Kinh was beaten to death, and the baby was taken off to stay at the temple.

When the villagers removed Thi Kinh's clothes to wash her body and bury her, they discovered she was a woman. Finally, they understood that she had been protecting the young girl, not wanting to shame or betray her. They revered Thi Kinh for the pain she had endured on behalf of another person.

Thi Kinh became a spirit then, and the spirit was Kwan Yin. Women found her story particularly moving; they looked up to her and prayed to her spirit. Women and men began to worship her.

Luong emphasizes, "There is no *magic* to Kwan Yin, only her extraordinary compassion that distinguishes her. The teaching is, not that she's a daughter of God— it just gives me a good example: look at this strength, and this patience! And now how many thousands of years later, women like me, my mother, my girlfriend burn incense every night for her!"

Luong has a shrine to Kwan Yin in her home in America. On the top shelf rests a statue of Kwan Yin, on the lower shelves are photographs of Luong's deceased relatives and her first husband. Each night she lights a stick of incense before Kwan Yin's image.

"Most Vietnamese women chant to Kwan Yin because we look up to her; she helps us get through the hard times," she says. "Kwan Yin helps me with a lot of the issues I have to deal with now. I try to practice what I have learned from her. Patience, compassion."

"Leaving Home"

For years I had heard about an old Asian *bhikshuni* (nun) who was considered to be a living embodiment of Kwan Yin. I thought she was Chinese and that she lived in Santa Cruz. But at Gold Mountain Monastery in San Francisco, I was told by one of the nuns that such a person lived in a monastery in San Jose and that she had come from Vietnam. Her name, I was told, is Heng Ji Sr.

One day I drove south on a crowded freeway to the good-sized city of San Jose. After much consulting of the map and several wrong turns, I found myself driving far into the outskirts of the city and up a small mountain. At its top, commanding a spectacular view of San Jose, stood a complex of low buildings that formerly had been a hospital for the disabled, complete with classrooms and an empty swimming pool. This was Gold Sage Monastery.

The woman at the desk of the reception area told us that ten or so *bhikshunis* currently live at the monastery. Gold Sage is one of the ten monasteries founded in the United States and Canada by the great Chinese Dharma Master Hsuan Hua, who died in 1995. The nuns and monks of this order all bear the name Heng, which means "true or real." They move from monastery to monastery as they are needed. But I was told that because of her age, Heng Ji lives at Gold Sage Monastery permanently. I was also told that her ten-year-old granddaughter was there with her, as a novice nun.

A tiny robed figure came down the corridor toward me. Heng Ji smiled delightedly when she saw me and hurried forward to clasp my fingers in her small, soft, cool hands. Her bright eyes welcomed me, as if she had known me forever. She wore the yellow under-robe and brown outer-robe of a fully ordained member of her order; her head was freshly shaven.

We went into a sort of parlor and sat on a couch together, as a helpful *bhikshuni* went off to find Gwo Ting, Heng Ji's granddaughter.

Heng Ji and I smiled at each other. The name Gwo Ting, she told me, means "beautiful fruit" in Vietnamese. She told me how Gwo Ting at age five had said to her, "I want to see the Buddha in heaven," and had asked to be allowed to become a nun. Her mother had allowed her to "leave home" at the age of six and take the robes of a novice nun. Leaving home has both literal and symbolic meaning, for a nun really has no earthly home and she lives always with the understanding of the impermanence of all phenomena, the groundlessness and emptiness of all existence.

Gwo Ting and another small novice burst into the room radiating curiosity and lively energy. The *bhikshuni* who went to collect her is, it turns out, their teacher, and she brought images of Kwan Yin for us to look at. The little girls pursue their lessons at the monastery and one day a week they go down the hill to a private elementary school in San Jose. I wonder what it is like for them in that setting, for both have shaved heads and wear full robes.

While we admire the pictures—prints of paintings, mostly—Gwo Ting now and then points out a detail for me, her black eyes throwing me a curious sideways glance. The little girls are very contained and reserved but with an open, sweet demeanor. And I sense from them also a playfulness just barely contained.

Soon the miniature nuns go off with their tutor to continue their studies. Heng Ji tells me Gwo Ting will probably not take her full precepts until she is twenty years old. I find myself impressed with this life of commitment taken on so young, and know that in our culture we have no comparable opportunity for a child to focus so strongly on spirituality.

Gwo Ting is not her only grandchild, Heng Ji explains. She has five daughters, two sons, and fourteen grandchildren.

She is happy to tell me about her relationship with Kwan Yin, beginning during the Second World War when the Japanese war planes came to "plant a bomb" on Saigon where she was living. Her grandmother chanted to Kwan Yin to rescue them, and they were saved. "We all have the Buddha nature," Heng Ji assures me. "Chanting the Great Compassion Mantra helps many things."

I am so relaxed sitting here with Heng Ji. In the presence of these nuns, one has the sense that all is well. And there is no distraction. Heng Ji, gentle, smiling, gives the impression of being entirely present in this moment and at the same time entirely empty—that is, having no agenda or intruding thoughts or desires. It's peaceful, cheerful, restful to be here with her.

Heng Ji tells me that during the Vietnam War she lived in Saigon with her husband, who was a military official. She prayed to Kwan Yin to keep him safe, and he survived many close shaves.

Five years after her husband's death in 1976, with several of her children she escaped Vietnam on a boat constructed by fishermen especially for this journey. With its cargo of fifty-three people, it set off for Indonesia, sailing four nights and three days. Partway on their journey a powerful wind came up, and the boat pitched and tossed, threatening to capsize. The people cried out in terror. Heng Ji chanted to Kwan Yin, asking her to save them, and gradually the wind calmed down. Still another night her son, who had no experience in sailing, tried to steer the boat. It seemed that something was pushing the boat very fast all night long, toward their destination and asylum. Could that have been Kwan Yin? For two nights Heng Ji heard the sound of someone reciting holy verses, but she did not see anybody doing it. Finally, they spotted land. They had arrived safely in Indonesia.

A year later Heng Ji was able to immigrate and make her way to the City of Ten Thousand Buddhas, a monastery in Northern California.

In 1984, Heng Ji "left home" and became a fully ordained *bhikshuni.*

As we have been talking, she has stroked and patted my hand, leaned toward me, smiled into my eyes. I feel completely content, as if I could sit here forever with her, but soon it is time to go.

As I take my leave of Heng Ji, the woman from the desk takes me into the meditation hall for a moment. There I see a beautiful wooden statue of the Thousand-Armed Guan Shih Yin. This manifestation of Kwan Yin began as the incarnation of the supposedly historical figure of Princess Miao Shan.

The legend of Miao Shan holds a very important place in the process of the feminization of Avalokite-svara/Kwan Yin that took place in ancient China. Of all the images of Kwan Yin, the Thousand-Armed Guan Shih Yin representations are closest in form to many of the images of the male Avalokitesvara. The thousand arms spread out in a sort of halo around the statue; in addition, there are forty-two larger arms, each holding a sacred implement used by Kwan Yin in her efforts to save and heal people. The statues typically have eleven heads, some fierce, some beneficent, so that Kwan Yin can look down from all angles on the world of human beings (see figure 1).

Princess Miao Shan

Miao Shan was born several thousand years ago, third daughter of a king and queen. Hers was a miraculous birth. At the moment of conception her mother had dreamed that she swallowed the moon; and then when the child was born, the earth shook and the smell of flowers filled the air. Miao Shan was a very beautiful baby, enveloped in a many-colored light, and everyone who saw her knew she was a goddess. But although they were parents of a divine being, her mother and father had wanted a son, and they were disappointed.

When Miao Shan grew into young adulthood, she

resisted her parents' insistence that she marry. She wanted to meditate and pray; she dressed simply and ate only rice and vegetables. Her kindness became so well-known that she was called the Maiden with the Heart of the Buddha.

Miao Shan's father tried to force her to marry, but she refused. He became incensed and decreed that she would have to do the dirtiest jobs in the palace and be given just enough food to survive. Her mother was so upset at this that she begged the king to send Miao Shan to a nunnery instead. The king agreed but decided he still wanted to teach Miao Shan a lesson. He visited the abbess of the nunnery and told her that she and her nuns should make life difficult and unpleasant for the princess, thinking that would make her more receptive to marriage.

The abbess made Miao Shan work at the humblest tasks in the kitchen. Miao Shan set to work cheerfully, but the heavy tasks weighed her down. Then the Master of Heaven, seeing her dilemma, sent deities and animals to help her. Birds gathered vegetables for her, tigers brought firewood, a dragon dug a well, and gods worked in the kitchen with her to complete her tasks.

When the king heard that Miao Shan's spirit had not been broken and that she still refused to marry, he became enraged again and ordered his soldiers to go to the nunnery, burn it down, and kill all the nuns. The soldiers marched to the nunnery and set it on fire, making sure that no nuns could escape the flames.

In the pandemonium as the nuns tried to escape, they turned in anger on Miao Shan, blaming her for what they saw as their imminent death. Miao Shan prayed to the Buddha to help them. Then she pricked the top of her mouth and spat blood into the air. It became vast rain clouds that poured water on the flames and doused them.

The king, hearing of this, ordered that his daughter be brought back to the palace in chains and executed. But the Master of Heaven made plans to foil him. When Miao Shan was led out into the square, a brilliant light opened around her and the executioner's sword broke into pieces. He picked up a spear with which to kill her, and the spear dissolved in his hand. Finally, he resorted to a silken cord, choking her to death.

Suddenly, a huge tiger bounded into the square and ran away with Miao Shan's dead body. The Earth God Tiger took her to a safe place and put a pill of immortality in her mouth. After some adventures in the world of the gods, Miao Shan came back to life and went to a mountain where she meditated for many years, perfecting her bodhisattva nature.

Her father did not do so well. As a result of his evil deeds, he became sick with numerous painful ailments. No doctor could help him. Then, when he was almost dead, a strange monk appeared and told him he could be saved. If he could "take the arm and eye of one who is without anger, combine them into a medicine, and apply it," he would be cured.

The king did not think he could find anyone who would make such a sacrifice for him, but the monk told him there was a person on a nearby mountain who would do this. So the king sent a messenger to Miao Shan. When Miao Shan heard of her father's plight, "she smiled upon the messenger, gouged out her eyes and cut off both arms, which she laid before the astonished and horrified messenger. As her offerings were gathered up, the whole Earth shook at the momentousness of these actions."

The king was cured by the potion made from this grisly offering. When he was well again, he and his queen went to give thanks to the person who had saved him. When they bowed before the mutilated woman, to their horror, they recognized her as Miao Shan, their daughter. The king, overcome, fell to the floor and asked her to forgive him.

With that, Miao Shan rose into the air and assumed the form of the Thousand-Armed and Thousand-Eyed Guan Shih Yin. She hovered above her parents for a time and then ascended into the clouds, radiating light. (From Palmer et al.)

This extravagant story has been carried down in song and legend, painting and carving, in China, in various more or less complicated versions, to this day.

In later retellings of the story of Miao Shan, according to Chün-fang Yü, she is portrayed in her divine aspect not as having a thousand arms and eyes "but rather as a normal woman holding a green willow branch in one arm and a bottle containing pure water or ambrosia in the other. . . ."

One frequently sees this image of Kwan Yin. Wearing a white robe, she sits at the water's edge holding a willow whisk or lotus blossom and her vial of sacred fluid. The fluid may be the elixir of life or it may be the balm of her compassion that she pours out onto the world (see figure 2).

The willow is the symbol of Buddhist virtues: It can bend in the most violent storms and come back into balance again. The "weeping willow" suggests compassion for the sorrows and suffering of the world. Also, the willow is an ancient Chinese symbol of femininity; because of its magical powers, it is used to exorcise demons and in the practice of shamanistic rituals.

Where She Lives

"If Kwan Yin lives anywhere in the United States, it's at City of Ten Thousand Buddhas," said a Chinese-American friend of mine.

I knew this to be true, because I had visited this unique Buddhist oasis in the timber country of Northern California several times. Now I was driving toward

Figure 2. In this representation of Kwan Yin pouring balm from her vial, she is a giant woman resting casually on a wooded mountain. I like her world-weary, I've-seen-it-all expression.

it again, on a sunny morning, hoping to speak with nuns and laywomen there.

As I drove north, I reflected on the history of City of Ten Thousand Buddhas. It is a huge complex of structures, many of them white stucco with orange-tiled roofs, built originally as a state institution to house the mentally ill. That was its function for a number of years until the water supply ran out and the hospital and other facilities had to close. Master Hua, the Chinese Buddhist teacher from San Francisco, and his students who wanted to buy the property were advised not to consider it because of this lack of water. But, as the story goes, Master Hua walked out on the land, pointed his stick at the ground, and ordered, "Dig here." They did and found a spring, which supplies ample water.

I enter the City through an ornate, pagoda-style triple gate and find myself in a compound shaded by old trees, below a clear blue sky, with mountains rising close behind. As I pull up next to the administration building of the Dharma Realm Buddhist University, a gorgeous peacock struts past, dragging his long-feathered tail across the grass. Giving a startling screech, he pauses and lifts his tail to fan out in the sunshine, dazzling me with its extravagant glossy colors. I know that the peacock's presence here carries more than ornamental significance.

Kwan Yin and the Peacock

In early times the world's creatures were misbehaving, and Kwan Yin came down out of the sky to teach them how to treat each other. As long as she was there watching them, they would be compassionate and loving toward one another, but when she left them to their own devices, they would argue and fight and treat each other badly again. Several times Kwan Yin arrived to chide and teach them and then left. Several times the creatures slipped back into their old destructive ways. Finally, Kwan Yin thought of a solution. She called to her a large bird of a dull brown color, who had very long tail feathers. Telling the other creatures that they needed someone to keep watch over them, she passed her hands over her face and then over the bird, whose plumage instantly transformed into brilliantly hued shining feathers. At the end of each tail feather was a bright clear eye that stared out at the other creatures. Kwan Yin told them her servant, the peacock, would watch over them with his eyes and report to her about their behavior. She then ascended into the heavens. It is said that the peacock struts because it is proud of its special role as Kwan Yin's servant and that its eyes remind us creatures of the world that Kwan Yin is watching over us. (From Palmer et al.)

The grounds of the City of Ten Thousand Buddhas contain a monastery, university, library, Buddhist text translation society, ordination hall, boys' school and girls' school, as well as many other buildings such as workshops, studios, and residence halls for the hundreds of pilgrims who come to meditate and chant; an eating hall; and even a public restaurant that serves delicious vegetarian food. At its center is the Buddha Hall (formerly an auditorium), which does literally contain ten thousand small buddha statues, each placed in a wooden niche in the wall, ranged from floor to ceiling. This great meditation and chanting hall is dominated by a huge, splendidly gilded statue of the Thousand-Armed Guan Shih Yin Bodhisattva (Kwan Yin), rising above the altar at its front (see figure 1).

Having been met by my guide Pamela Haines, a new arrival at the City, I am led into the Buddha Hall, where a repentance ceremony is taking place. This ceremony, which consists mostly of chanting and bowing, goes on for many weeks, each day, all day. Hundreds of people are gathered in the hall, standing in rows, many in the robes of *bhikshus* (monks) and *bhikshunis* (nuns). The other rows are occupied mostly by women wearing ordinary street clothes.

In the middle, between the two rows of participants, stands the abbot. He is a young Chinese man of impressive height, draped in a splendid orange silk robe, who stands so still that I think he is a statue—until he bows.

Pamela and I take our places in a row and look at the chant book opened on a music stand before us. We chant a phrase, five or six Chinese syllables looping in an ornate melody line. Then we bow. Pamela has shown me how. We bend down, put hands to the padded stool, then knees, then head down on the stool. Stay there, open hands. Let everything go. What a relief it is—for just a moment—to empty myself. Then we stand up and sing another phrase.

A small young woman takes her place beside me. (Pamela has pointed her out to me beforehand as a teacher in the girls' elementary school, who works tirelessly and never sleeps.) This person, not five feet tall, wears trousers (as do all the other women, trousers being the usual Chinese female dress), a white shirt,

and a tan vest with "Dharma Realm University"
imprinted in a circle on the back. With her tiny callused
hand she points out each syllable for me so that I can
chant with the others. The text is written in Chinese
characters with the transliteration next to each; it reads
from right to left. Without this helper, I would be completely lost; with her hand pointing out the syllables,
I chant a bit raggedly, following the melody the others
are singing. Now and then she leaves me to help someone who has just come in or who looks confused. Then
she's back, her finger finding the syllable for me. She is
steady as a rock during the two thirty-minute chanting
and bowing sessions that I attend.

I have looked at the gorgeous statues for sale in the
gift shop. Kwan Yin standing, all in white, holding a
baby. Kwan Yin pouring sacred fluid from her vial.
Kwan Yin seated, holding the stem of a lotus flower, her
robe gilded. Kwan Yin standing with the Buddha and
another bodhisattva. And before me in the meditation
hall is the giant, Thousand-Armed Guan Shih Yin at
the center of the altar rising up majestic and spiky with
bronze-gold hands. But the bodhisattva herself also
stands next to me, patiently pointing out each sound
so that I can chant with the others.

Many of the participants at this retreat, and the
majority of the students who attend the schools, are Chinese who have traveled from various parts of Asia. The
City of Ten Thousand Buddhas is renowned in Asia and
considered a pilgrimage site.

Each year, usually in July or August (the dates are
chosen from the Chinese lunar calendar), the Festival of
Guan Shih Yin is celebrated here with a whole week of

ceremony and recitation of the name Guan Yin. The week begins with a purification ceremony in which the Great Compassion mantra is chanted; the next day is a celebration of Guan Yin Bodhisattva's enlightenment. The week proceeds with day-long chanting and bowing to Guan Yin. Participants recite the "Universal Door Chapter" of the Lotus Sutra twice a day; the rest of the time they chant "Namo Guan Shi Yin Pu-Sa," the name of the bodhisattva. This is a mantra, words that go beyond their literal meaning to hold a power in themselves, their recitation taking one to a level beyond conceptual thought. This chant is said to be the most powerful means of invoking Guan Yin. And when it is recited in this week-long session, one's consciousness, as John Blofeld has noted, "borne aloft by the flow of mantric sound, soars upwards to a sphere of marvelous luminosity."

The culmination of the festival to Kwan Yin is the recitation of her name, in the chant *Namo Guan Shih Yin Pu-Sa* (Hail to Kwan Yin Bodhisattva), over and over. The tempo progresses from slow to fast and brings the assembled participants into a line to snake throughout the Buddha Hall, eventually almost at a running pace. The hours of this retreat not spent in the Buddha Hall are given to silence, so that participants can continue the recitation of Kwan Yin's name in their minds as they eat and wash and prepare to sleep.

Pamela and I sit with two *bhikshunis* at a picnic table on the lawn. One is a Western woman, wearing glasses, looking studious and yet cheerful with her shaven head and brown and orange robes. A Chinese nun, who has

an aura of authority, also sits with us. Both of these
women have been ordained as *bhikshunis* for many
years. The City of Ten Thousand Buddhas is a very
strict monastic establishment founded on the *Vinaya*
(the monastic rules set down by the Buddha). Men and
women are kept separate. The monks and nuns practice
meditation, precepts, mantras and mudras (hand ges-
tures), and other esoteric practices, as well as studying,
memorizing, reciting, and lecturing on the canonical
texts. Anyone living on the property, for whatever reason, is required to follow the daily schedule of practices. Major chants performed each day are addressed to
Guan Shih Yin Bodhisattva and sing her praises, so that
she is kept strongly in everyone's consciousness.

Respecting the "leaving home" vows of these nuns,
I agree not to reveal any details of their personal lives
before becoming *bhikshunis* or even to identify them.
A hallmark of the homeless life is leaving behind the
individual ego. These nuns are integrated into and well
taken care of in this Chinese Mahayana environment;
it is entirely appropriate that they would not want to
call attention to themselves as individuals.

Opened on the table before us lies *The Dharani Sutra,*
with its pictures of the many manifestations of Kwan
Yin, each corresponding to a line of the mantra. Kwan
Yin appears on one page as a beautiful maiden riding
on a lion-like creature, on another page as a fierce male
warrior with a sword, yet again as a female sage seated
in meditation and holding a lotus blossom. We are dis-
cussing how Kwan Yin will show herself in a body to
speak the Dharma.

"To different people Guan Yin will appear a different

way," says the Western nun. "If the person needs to see Guan Yin as a *bhikshu* or *bhikshuni* or as a layman or laywoman, as a king or a minister or a housewife, then that is how she will appear. The Universal Door chapter of the Lotus Dharma Flower Sutra mentions thirty-two ways that Gwan Yin has of responding to people. These are just ways of categorizing: in reality it's infinite variations. The chapter also describes various situations where a person would call on Guan Yin Bodhisattva out of a need, and Guan Yin Bodhisattva would respond. But in that case, Guan Yin Bodhisattva would not necessarily appear in a certain kind of body. For example, if someone was pushing you off a cliff, Guan Yin bodhisattva would catch you."

"And what form would she be in?" I ask.

"You might not see her."

The Chinese nun explains, "You feel this force catching you." And I recall Heng Ji's telling of the great force that seemed to be pushing the boat through the night when she and her family were escaping from Vietnam.

The Western nun continues, "There are many, many stories, in Chinese, true accounts. Sometimes they'll say, 'This person was attacking me and I called out Guan Yin Bodhisattva's name and the person looked up and he went, "Ahhh," and then he ran away.' " She laughs. "You know, you couldn't see anyone, but the person who was attacking you could see that there was something there. So sometimes Guan Yin Bodhisattva will appear in a very fierce-looking manifestation to do that—to frighten, for the purpose of saving."

They tell about the Vietnamese refugee resettlement program they ran here at City, caring for the refugees,

teaching them English and marketable skills, preparing
them to take their place in American society. And they
recount some of the stories of the people on the boats
who called Kwan Yin's name and were rescued.

But the nuns emphasize that for them Kwan Yin,
while certainly a salvific figure in the external world,
functions more as an aid to their spiritual work. "The
thing that I request from Guan Yin is that she help me
to get rid of my hatred," says the Western nun. "The
same with greed and ignorance. The three poisons. In
other words, Guan Yin Bodhisattva helps us with our
practice. So she's working at every conceivable level."

The Chinese nun interjects, "And she works in different realms."

"The ultimate aim is to teach and transform the person so he or she can practice and become enlightened."

We look at the dramatic drawings of Kwan Yin's
many manifestations in the book and discuss them,
while peacocks screech somewhere across the lawn.
A snow-white bird spreads his magnificent tail for us
in the sunlight.

I want to know how these two women, who have
committed their lives to spiritual practice, view these
visions of Kwan Yin.

The Chinese nun answers, "To realize our own Buddha form."

And the Western nun elaborates, "It's more than simply venerating a being outside. Our teacher would often
say, 'If you recite Guan Yin's name sincerely, then you
will become Guan Yin. You and Guan Yin will become
one.' And he would say things like, 'Guan Yin Bodhisattva is our relative.' Throughout the cosmos in the

Great Vehicle, Buddhism, there are many worlds, many buddhas, and many different kinds of living beings. But in this particular world Guan Yin Bodhisattva has her special conditions with people, so many people when they meet up with Guan Yin Bodhisattva are not surprised; they actually feel a familiarity."

Familiar Energy

To come of Chinese background is to know about Kwan Yin, even if your parents do not revere her. In the house in South Central Los Angeles where Phyllis Pay grew up, there was no Kwan Yin figure. Her grandparents set up a small altar to the ancestors when someone died, but no deities were displayed. And her mother, a divorced woman who worked in a factory to support her two children, never mentioned Kwan Yin.

But when Phyllis first encountered Kwan Yin, "it just felt very familiar, like something I'd always known. I didn't have to ask myself, What does Kwan Yin represent? or who is she? or why is she holding this vase?—it just feels like something that was embedded in my consciousness. That's a very strong archetypal figure. It's like it's always been there in the background and so you don't question, when you make contact with it, it's just *there*."

Phyllis Pay earns her living as a psychic reader and counselor. She is the founder and director of The Intuitive Energy Center in Berkeley, which offers everything from intuition training to men's and women's groups, to classes in meditation, movement, and mediation. Phyllis's life intersects frequently with those of her children—her son who has just become a lawyer, her daughter who is studying to become an acupuncturist. She practices Tibetan Buddhism and, with the Buddhist scholar Anne Klein, has led a pilgrimage to the sacred caves of Tibet. It was Phyllis who went with me to Pu To Island to encounter Kwan Yin on her own Chinese territory.

We talk in Phyllis's home, at a table where she has placed several of her Kwan Yin statues for me to examine. Particularly interesting is a boxed plaster figure with long snaky hair, made by a New Mexico artist, Susan Charlot Jay.

Phyllis gives the impression of strong attention and presence as we talk. She is a short, round-faced woman who listens intently and thinks before she speaks.

Her mother, she tells me, was born here, but her mother's older half-brother had been born in China. Her mother attended a Christian church when she was young, as some Christians in Los Angeles had directed their missionary zeal to the Chinese community. "But she never really adopted Christianity."

When Phyllis came upon Kwan Yin, she did not discuss her discovery with her mother, but she knew that her mother was familiar with Kwan Yin. She also knew very well why her mother had never mentioned this Chinese embodiment to her.

Phyllis's mother had good reason to suppress any evidence of her Chinese spiritual background, as the necessity to assimilate into American society in the 1940s when she was young seemed crucial. World War Two raged in Europe and the Pacific; the Chinese immigrants watched as their Japanese neighbors were taken from their homes, their goods were confiscated, and they were sent off to internment camps. They lived in fear.

"I was born right after the war, and so I grew up in the fifties; but the memory of that happening was in my mother, so assimilation seemed much more important in those days than it does now."

Now Phyllis's mother keeps a Kwan Yin statue in her house, along with the classic Chinese longevity figures, such as the old man carrying a peach.

Fingering a handsome, small, carved-wood Kwan Yin, Phyllis speaks of the bodhisattva as having been "in the background" throughout her life. "I can't say when I consciously came into contact with Kwan Yin, but when I did it just was taken for granted that she really does exist. I think Kwan Yin is a representation of the divine mother." In her daily practice she chants Kwan Yin mantras, in conjunction with mantras to other female deities and a contemporary female Hindu saint. "I do those mantras every day to stay connected to that energy. I think when you are receptive to guidance or help from that level it just automatically is there, in whatever form you want to receive it."

In her work as a psychic counselor, Phyllis calls upon Kwan Yin not so much as an active element who occasions breakthroughs but for general solace and compassion. "I have in my mind different kinds of energies connected with different deities that I actually work with, and to me Kwan Yin is wide compassion and open acceptance in the background."

"Just for yourself, do you sometimes petition her?" I ask, and she replies without hesitation.

"I do it on a daily basis. If you do that, things don't seem to move to crisis. It's not like waiting and waiting until there's crisis and *then* calling on Kwan Yin.

"And if there is something that's really bothering me, I specifically make a request about that. Whether it's for resolution or the highest good or highest purpose, something like that. If there's someone I know who is needing help, I would say the mantras and dedicate them to that person and do a visualization of Kwan Yin connecting to him or her, like an energy line going between Kwan Yin and that person. Usually, the Kwan Yin I'm visualizing is the one who is riding on the dragon through the ocean waves" (see figure 3).

As we put away the statues, Phyllis tells me there is a particular experience on Pu To Island that she wants to share. Pu To Shan means "sacred mountain." It is a small island in an archipelago in the South China Sea several hours' boat ride from Shanghai. For hundreds of years this island has been dedicated to Kwan Yin; before the devastation wrought by the Red Guards in the Cultural Revolution, it was the site of hundreds of temples—now there are just a few; it is said that Kwan Yin resides on Pu To Island and that going there may occasion a meeting with her. The island is also a prime tourist spot, with a million tourists per year coming from mainland China, Taiwan, Hong Kong, and the Philippines, to lie on the beaches and eat at the excellent fish restaurants.

It is particularly the Kwan Yin of the South Sea who is venerated on Pu To Island. She is generally seen riding through the waves on a sea monster or giant fish. Classically, she has two attendants, one young woman,

Figure 3. Kwan Yin riding a dragon through ocean waves. This image is purported to be an actual photograph taken by a passenger on a ship tossing in a storm.

Lung-nu, daughter of the Dragon King; the other a
young male pilgrim called Shan-tsai (in Sanskrit, Su-
dhana), whose travels to many teachers are recorded in
the Avatamsaka Sutra. And she is accompanied by a
white parrot. This Kwan Yin rescues sailors from ship-
wreck. She is probably the ancestor of local sea goddesses who reigned in the bays and inlets of Southern
China for centuries before Buddhism. Pilgrims go to Pu
To Island hoping to have a vision of her, which will
answer all their prayers and bring salvation to them
(see figure 4).

On this sacred island, crowded with tourists, we
felt the presence of Kwan Yin, not necessarily in the
famous caves or the temples but just in the cicadas buzz-
ing above our heads in the trees, in the humid heat, in
the rocks on which we would sit to rest. And here Phyllis had a powerful dream.

"The dream I had on the first night was so absolutely
vivid and such a powerful release that I feel I could
only have had it on Pu To Island, where the presence of
Kwan Yin is so strong. It had to do with a friend who
had died two and a half months before. It wasn't even
like a dream, it was more like an astral experience,
where she appeared to me and she was surrounded by
light, she was like an angel. I felt like it was Kwan Yin
who allowed this contact to happen. And my friend
told me that she loved me, and I started sobbing and telling her how much I missed her. She said she was all
right and that she had passed over. It was such a vivid
contact that it flooded me with a sense of acceptance of
her death. I experienced resolution, and solace. I felt
that only could have happened with Kwan Yin being
present."

南海普陀山觀世音菩薩聖像

Figure 4. Kwan Yin in one of her manifestations on Pu To Island. This cloth is imprinted with an image taken from a famous stele on the island. It is bought by pilgrims, who have it stamped at each temple they visit. Note the three ornate square stamps to either side and above Kwan Yin's head, each giving the name of a temple on the island.

After the dream Phyllis came down with a fever, and while she knows there were physical reasons for her illness, she also thinks the illness had another purpose. "To consciously open to a certain level of compassion, I had to release some of my own judgments, either judgments in reference to myself or judgments that I hold in general as defensive mechanisms. That release process was stimulated earlier on by wanting to go to the island and physically make contact with bringing the compassion that Kwan Yin represents into my own body. And I think my getting sick was part of the release."

I ask Phyllis about the influence of Kwan Yin on her work, and she explains to me that her path and her training has been in Western metaphysics, learning how to use psychic work. But her own growth in that work, and because she has a background in psychology as well, has led her to use psychic perception as a way of facilitating personal growth.

"So it's not used to predict the future or perpetuate illusion," she tells me, "it's to break through illusion and break down structures and to use psychic perception as a way of reading people's pictures, and the pictures being their illusions. So what you're trying to do is to clear energy, to clear space, so that people become more open and grounded. I work a lot with grounding.

"It feels as if somewhere along the path I really needed to bring the element of compassion into my work. If you're going to go deeply with people in terms of energetic perception and going beyond certain layers in order to bring to the surface sometimes very strongly repressed material or things that have been very painful, you have to do that with compassion.

How to do that from the heart? This is part of the evolutionary process of using the kind of powers that Western metaphysics has developed over time; first, you learn the techniques, then you bring in the element of the heart, which is the element of compassion. Which is where my contact with Kwan Yin was really important. It's almost like I had to bring Kwan Yin through my heart in order to balance the power of the work in terms of awakening. If you're going to awaken people, you have to have a container for how the work can happen. And so Kwan Yin has been extremely important as an energy that I have brought through my heart as a sense of compassion."

She shows me the bracelet on her arm, a string of shiny beads bearing Kwan Yin's name. "So what happens is when I even think about Kwan Yin—and I have this bracelet so she's always with me—I reference her compassion in my heart. If you're sitting in contact with somebody and something painful is going on, the place where you want to sit is in the heart. Focusing on Kwan Yin and doing prayers to Kwan Yin actually opens the heart and makes it available to you. If you're sitting there and your heart is not available, if you call upon Kwan Yin then the heart becomes available. As a daily practice, that's how the presence is always with me. And that's how I work with people."

A Problematical Relationship

While European-Americans come to Kwan Yin freely and incorporate her into their lives, the relationship of Asian and Asian-American women to this powerful

figure can be more complicated. Phyllis Pay points out
that the determining word associated with Kwan Yin
is "self-sacrifice," a capacity that is highly valued in
Asian women. An Asian-American woman seeking to
make her way in the aggressive, secular world of modern America, and yet bound in many ways by the expectations of her ethnic background, may feel inhibited by
the values associated with Kwan Yin and may reject the
figure of Kwan Yin herself.

Questions are raised, then, about how religion and
the veneration of Kwan Yin have contributed to the
oppression of women. In China women chant with
great energy and even desperation to Kwan Yin to give
them a male child, while little girl babies are left at the
doors of orphanages. From a feminist or Western perspective, is this a beneficial "use" of Kwan Yin?

One Asian-born woman, who has opted to remain
anonymous, tells me that Kwan Yin was the most popular deity in her country when she was growing up. In
the downtown of her city there was a special Kwan Yin
temple. Her uncle was a city official in that district, and
so the family felt a special affinity for this temple. The
temple survived burning, earthquake, war, and other
disasters, and this Kwan Yin always protected the
family from misfortunes.

This woman, whom I will call Noriko, tells of her
mother's and her aunts' strong relationship with the
Kwan Yin statue. Often they took the young Noriko to
the temple. Recently, when her father was dying, Noriko again visited the temple to pray and realized that
the statue she had always thought of as big, was actually very small, just a few inches tall. "Just the thought

that the city was protected by this small Kwan Yin moved me tremendously," she says.

When Noriko was growing up, her mother was an attractive, full-bodied woman, and she was so generous that some people thought she resembled Kwan Yin. So Noriko's impression of Kwan Yin was always associated with the image of her mother, and she has a very close relationship with Kwan Yin. "When I need help," she says, "I always call on Kwan Yin. At the high Buddhist levels Kwan Yin is a male, or neutral, but at the folk level she appears as a woman and a women's protector. In our patriarchal culture, we needed somebody to cling to, somebody to help us."

Noriko admits that Kwan Yin is, however, not her favorite deity because she reminds her too much of her real mother.

"You know, it must be very hard for educated Western Christian women to go back to Mary," she says. "It's exactly the same for me with Kwan Yin. She's a little stale, because she's over-used, and I have too many associations with her." Noriko had to struggle against her family's expectations for her. Her grandmother, a religious/political revolutionary, had died when Noriko's father was a child; she, too, had been viewed as a manifestation of Kwan Yin. "My father was so young when she died that he made this woman into an ideal, and he put that ideal on me, that I should become a selfless person." This expectation caused her years of conflict as she tried to establish her identity.

She points out that Kwan Yin practice often can ignore the "dark side" of life. I am reminded of Phyllis Pay's pointing out that in the popular response to Kwan

Yin all is light and compassion, with no acknowledg-
ment of the more difficult aspects of human nature.
Both of them express the uneasiness some Asian
women feel about the image and influence of Kwan
Yin, their ambivalence fueled by long cultural and
personal/familial history.

Kwan Yin in Burma

Of the many Dharma teachers I have known, Thynn
Thynn strikes me as the most steadfast and unfailingly
warm. Dr. Thynn Thynn, a retired physician, a mother
of two grown children, a meditator, and a teacher who
inspires confidence and strong commitment, was born
and lived most of her life in Burma. She herself is ethni-
cally Chinese and grew up near the Burma/Thai border,
but her meditation training and early experience were
Burmese.

Thynn Thynn, bespectacled and usually smiling,
gives you a hug and inquires about your health and
your family and all your doings. One can think of her
as a concerned mother or aunt, but not for long. In her
teaching sessions, she will fix you with a strongly
focused look, then ask a question that pierces all your
defenses and turns you inward. Thynn Thynn focuses
you always toward your own wisdom, sets you inquir-
ing about your own path and capacities.

I have known Thynn Thynn for ten years, having
heard about her first when she was teaching in Bangkok. A very discerning and intelligent Western woman
who was living as a nun in Bangkok told me she had
found a teacher who cut through all the obscuration

and pointed to the truth. Later, Thynn Thynn began to appear in California settings, giving talks, and leading meditations, journeying from her home in Scarsdale, New York, where she was living with her family. Finally, she moved to Sebastopol in Northern California, where a community has gathered around her, and together they are working to establish a residential center for individual meditators and families. The center they envision will maintain a strong relationship with the community at large; they plan to offer outreach programs, such as free clinics and other services, and to provide a haven for the old, infirm, and disadvantaged. Thynn Thynn has always insisted that Buddhist practice be integrated into daily life, amid all the busyness and challenges of work and family. This she emphasizes in her public lectures and meditation classes.

Recently, Thynn Thynn told me about her relationship with Kwan Yin, who proved to be very instrumental in creating the interest that is now being shown in her work. Some years ago she collected some question-and-answer excerpts of her lectures to publish in a little book. The Kwan Yin (Chuang Yen) temple in Carmel, New York, near her home at the time, donated the money for this first publication, and thus the modest paperback *Living Meditation, Living Insight* was produced (see Books and Articles). This volume has traveled over the world. The book has found its way into many places and occasioned many invitations and opportunities for Thynn Thynn to give the Dharma. For example, it was reprinted in Taiwan and sent to Australia, where an Australian Buddhist found it, and from this contact Thynn Thynn was invited to lecture and teach in Australia, which she now does regularly. Thynn Thynn considers that Kwan Yin had a serious hand in spreading the word.

But an earlier experience, in Burma, convinced Thynn Thynn that the bodhisattva had her interests in mind. At the time she had one daughter and was pregnant with a second child. Her husband was distressed, as he was trying to resign from his government job and had applied to the United States as an immigrant. He had not been accepted yet, so the family was in an insecure, in-between period. Thynn Thynn's method of birth control had failed, so the child was conceived accidentally. Her husband did not want to leave her and go to the United States while she was pregnant. All seemed difficult and insoluble.

Thynn Thynn had been visiting a Burmese Dharma-writer, who had a statue of Kwan Yin in his house. With her brother she had gone there several times to discuss Zen with this scholar.

Then Thynn Thynn had a dream. Kwan Yin appeared to her in a form very like the statue in the writer's home and said, "I would like to come to your house and be with you. But you've got to recognize and venerate me in the right way." Thynn Thynn woke up, thinking the dream had been a result of the morning sickness she had been having. Not taking it seriously, she went back to sleep. Again she fell into a dream, in which she saw her husband's face beaming with happiness. Then Kwan Yin appeared and said, "If you perform a small ritual, if you recognize me as a guardian, your husband's affairs will be taken care of."

When Thynn Thynn told her husband of the dream,

he was elated. They sought the advice of an older woman married to a Chinese man, who showed Thynn Thynn how to arrange a small altar and do a ritual with flowers and incense. In her mind, she tried to visualize and connect with Kwan Yin.

Within a week, Thynn Thynn's husband got his resignation from his government post, which is what he had needed before he could move ahead with plans for immigration.

Thynn Thynn's brother went to visit the Dharmawriter and told him what had happened. The Dharmawriter insisted that the brother take his statue of Kwan Yin and bring it back to Thynn Thynn's house. At first the brother refused, for he was traveling by bus and was afraid of damaging the statue, but his companion convinced him to wrap up and carry the statue back to Thynn Thynn.

They set up this image of Kwan Yin on the altar they had created and surrounded her with offerings of flowers, incense, and fruits. The whole extended family came to pay respects to her. Thynn Thynn's brother, who was learning to paint, did a number of paintings of this Kwan Yin to give to the relatives. Even Thynn Thynn's mother became Kwan Yin's devotee.

Several months later, her husband's visa for the United States was delayed. Then, when Thynn Thynn was seven months pregnant, she had a session with a clairvoyant. This person said that she saw Kwan Yin standing behind Thynn Thynn, saying, "This child was given to you as a gift. He will be a boy [which was true] and will bring prosperity to the family. Greater than the parents together he will be. Take good care of him."

She specified that until the child was born, the father was to take no alcohol, red meat, or sex with other women.

After the birth, in the hospital in Rangoon, Thynn Thynn was put in a room facing the Shwedagong pagoda with its spectacular golden dome and spire. Each morning she watched a huge red sun come up behind the pagoda. A voice in her head repeated, *"Tet Nay Lin,"* which means "rising sun." And so Tet Nay Lin became her son's name.

"All along," Thynn Thynn tells me, "I have been guided by visions and dreams in how to take care of him."

So Thynn Thynn brings to her students a complex integration of her very modern engaged-in-the-world self, her deep Dharma penetration and practice, and her gifts from Burmese culture, where she first encountered Kwan Yin and became her devotee.

Oh Goddess, Give Us Strength to Cut Through

A woman who has created many images of Kwan Yin is the Japanese-born artist Mayumi Oda. While she is best-known for her beautiful silk screens of goddesses, many of them drawn from Buddhist sources, her passionate concerns extend to world politics. In the last decade she founded Plutonium Free Future, an organization of Japanese people working toward nuclear nonproliferation and the development of alternative energy sources, and Rainbow Serpent, a women's network addressing nuclear dangers. Most recently,

Mayumi has been teaching both meditation and women's leadership for Asian-American and Pacific-American women; and in Japan she teaches mostly women in meditation and self-inquiry.

On the day I arrive to talk with her in her low sprawling house near Muir Beach, Mayumi's garden spills over with spectacular color, and I am reminded of her many silk screens of garden vegetables. I stop for a moment at the pond to admire the gorgeous, fully open, pale yellow lotus blossoms.

Mayumi greets me in the yard. She is a small-boned woman in her fifties with an air at once of peacefulness and focused intensity. Inside the house, she makes green tea in a small pot and sets out cookies.

I am most curious about the silk screen she made of Kwan Yin astride a dragon, holding a sword (see figure 5). This image she calls "Goddess, Give Us Strength to Cut Through."

Mayumi speaks passionately about this Kwan Yin. "It's about taking care of yourself! We have so confused compassion with sympathy. Compassion is really the understanding of the whole world as one, that there's no separation between me and you. If you just give and give and give because you have sympathy, you're not taking care of *yourself,* and then you're not taking care of the whole world either. Women are trained to give away our own selves so much that it's very, very difficult for us to take ruthless action. But if you just give and give, in the end you become a very angry person and you don't know why you're angry. Unconsciously, it bubbles up. When this anger seizes you, it's dangerous. I realized I would have to be able to

Figure 5. Kwan Yin with Sword, or "Goddess, Give Us
Strength to Cut Through." Silk screen by Mayumi Oda.

say no to certain things, which was very difficult for me.

"I gave my Kwan Yin the sword of wisdom and ruthless action. So that I can cut through that kind of bullshit sympathy and allow my real self to act. And so that I can really take care of myself, too. And taking care of *myself* is taking care of others."

She tells about the dragon Kwan Yin rides on. "The dragon is a very auspicious, imaginary creature, who lives in a watery area, the clouds. Kwan Yin is not a real human, so it's just very appropriate that she rides on a dragon, it's her animal."

We talk about an early image Mayumi made of Kwan Yin riding on a bird. She says she did not know she was painting Kwan Yin. She thought she was painting the goddess inside her. "I was very inspired by a woman writer, Kanoko Okamoto. She was a tantric Buddhist, and she wrote about the practice of Kwan Yin. When I read her poems, I realized that what I was painting was Kwan Yin."

At the time Mayumi had been living in Princeton with her husband and two sons. This was before she had begun Buddhist practice. She was involved in a difficult transition, trying to discover her own path. The image of Kwan Yin that she created helped her find herself.

More recently, she has created a very traditional image of Kwan Yin. "I made a white-clothed Kwan Yin sitting under a willow tree. It felt good to do that. A friend of mine pinned her print at her bedside when she was dying. She passed away at night, and when the people with her looked out the window, there was the same moon as in the picture, shining on a tree just as it does there. My friend had been a very giving person."

We discuss how in this traditional image, Kwan Yin appears peaceful and non-doing. And Mayumi says, "It's just an emanation of love."

Through her artistic renderings, and through her practice of reading the sutra to Kwan Yin from the Lotus Sutra, Mayumi has come to an understanding of this goddess's significance for her.

"The more I get close to her, the more I realize that she is really a buddha within ourselves, she's not really outside. I'm very interested in her name—Kwan Yin and Avalokita—the Kwan is a very interesting Chinese character, it's 'seeing,' and the character 'yin' is a sound. Sometimes it's translated 'the one who sees the world cry.' And the other translation, into Japanese, 'Kan Ji zai bosatsu,' that's more like the way that she manifests very freely. It shows two sides of her, that she hears your cries and she manifests.

"But to me the practice to Kwan Yin is like seeing oneself in the mirror and finding the buddha figure there. And so you're aligning with that—you try to become Kwan Yin. In that action she really manifests and saves you and protects you, because she's with you and she's actually you. So that kind of practice has been very strong for me. Rather than putting her outside, it's trying to find her within ourselves.

"She becomes one, completely one. And that's why this Kwan Yin is our mirror, helping us open ourselves to the understanding of the nature of reality, that we and the outside world are not separate and, therefore, all action we take has its effect on other mortals."

Mayumi Oda's several beautiful silk screens of Kwan Yin exemplify this interconnectedness, for they have appeared on book covers and brochures, leaflets and greeting cards, T-shirts and banners, giving many Westerners their first opportunity to see an image of this magnetic goddess. Mayumi's efforts to envision and identify with Kwan Yin have given us images that can awaken our imagination, spark our interest, and perhaps open the door to a comforting and life-enhancing relationship with one who hears our cries.

Three: She Carries Me

She is a boat, she is a light
High on a hill in dark of night.
She is a wave, she is the deep,
She is the dark where angels sleep.
When all is still and peace abides,
She carries me to the other side.

(song) Jennifer Berezan

The women in this section came upon Kwan Yin in various ways; they saw a statue owned by a friend, read
a book, studied the art of tattoo. Something in them
responded to the goddess/bodhisattva, and from
then on she became a teacher, friend, savioress, who
appeared in their lives as a source of comfort and inspiration. A sincere student of the Dharma found help
from Kwan Yin when her small daughter almost died.
One woman channeled communications from Kwan
Yin. They pay tribute to her in a number of ways: a
singer/songwriter has produced a CD of a chant to
Kwan Yin; a poet has written a poem about Kwan Yin
and a prostitute; still another woman has placed a
permanent reminder of Kwan Yin on her skin; and a
teacher and author bottles a "Kwan Yin essence" made
from flowers and gemstones.

Each of these women brings the spirit of Kwan Yin

into our world. What she represents to them begins with female power and presence. She may remind them to cultivate compassion, to be of service, and to listen. She may support them in being politically active, acknowledging our connectedness to all beings. She may seem like a guardian angel; she may work to soften the heart and create more acceptance of oneself and others. And she may be helpful in the adoption and raising of a Chinese baby girl.

Whatever her function, Kwan Yin appears very vibrantly in the lives of these women, a familiar and cherished figure.

A Catholic Opens Her Heart

Marylou Ledwell has been a cabinet maker for twenty years. She lives in a sunny one-bedroom apartment in an old building on Broadway in Oakland. While we drink tea, she describes what it was like growing up in Massachusetts in the fifties, where she attended Catholic schools, including Regis College in Weston, Massachusetts, whose hilltop campus was dubbed "the virgin bastille." Marylou, a slender cheerful-looking fifty-three-year-old, chuckles as she tells me about it.

She first encountered Kwan Yin at the home of a friend whom she views as her bodhisattva. "She has a lot of fun, she plays; she's got a freedom that I don't see in too many people—that I aspire to."

Marylou's friend had a bronze Kwan Yin statue, very beautiful, very detailed, that she kept on an altar at the foot of her bed. "She told me a little bit about Kwan Yin. Her name, and I can't remember what else. But I was

instantly attracted. My impression was that she was a
guardian angel, somebody who would watch over us.
I think it just filled a void. I was definitely searching
for a more feminine face of god. So I really latched on
to her."

Marylou had rejected her Catholicism when she
moved from New England to California in the sixties.
But she is not put off by the parallels between Kwan Yin
and the Virgin Mary.

"Kwan Yin certainly is real familiar. The virgin was
seen as an intercessor, somebody who was more accessible than God the Father. And also more than Christ.
She was not a deity, not a god or a goddess. She was
somebody you could go to, you know [she speaks
timorously], 'Would you talk to God for me?' kind
of thing." She laughs.

"But Kwan Yin stood by herself. She wasn't a go-
between. And I don't see her as a god, either, but as
the figure of an enlightened being full of compassion.
An ideal. And there are no rules attached to her that I
know of. My understanding is that she's just there to
help, she's there to comfort people and to ease their
suffering."

Kwan Yin is very often viewed as a goddess of the
people, as Marylou sees her, rather than a Buddhist
deity. And her resemblance to the Virgin Mary, particularly in her white-robed form, comes from the influence
of early Christians who went to China bringing their
statues of the virgin. Nestorian Christians were the first
to arrive, being welcomed into China in the seventh
century c.e. In the late sixteenth century Jesuits from
Spain and Portugal came to China, bringing late Renais-

sance statues of the Madonna and child; and Chinese artists and porcelain makers used these images as models for their Kwan Yin statues.

Marylou says her prayer to Kwan Yin is to "ask her to help me be compassionate to myself, because I have a merciless mind. I have a very strong judge in me from my Catholic upbringing. So that's what she is for me. She helps me remember to be kind to myself. Soften to myself."

On the mantel in her living room Marylou has created an altar. When she does stretches in the morning she faces her Kwan Yin statue, feeling her connection to this figure. And recently the altar became even more important to her, as Marylou was diagnosed with lung cancer.

We look now at the collage tacked to the mirror behind the figure of Kwan Yin. It was made by Marylou's brother, with pictures of healthy lungs and photographs of Marylou over the years, before she was ill (see figure 6).

"See the bottom right picture? Just in the last few days I realize I look a little bit like my Kwan Yin there, with my eyebrows up, eyes closed, that smile."

Her brother sent a color Xerox of the collage to everyone in her family. Above it is a scroll that says, "The only important thing right now is to heal yourself," a message from Marylou's male companion to keep her focused where she can do the most good.

Marylou tells about the healing ritual she performed. "I had a Kwan Yin altar set up at my shop. So she presided over the festivities. That's when I put those stars around her, and they've been there since."

Figure 6. Marylou Ledwell's altar.

In Kwan Yin's hand is a button stamped OK. When I ask about it Marylou tells about coming to a point in her life when she could give up being a perfectionist and just allow herself to be a human being. For her ritual she made an effigy of her self-hating part, "the part of me that is mean to me—I tried to make it as ugly as I could and filled it with roses and candy and these OK buttons which I made. Little wooden buttons. One day, I realized that even my healing didn't need to be perfect. Nothing needed to be perfect. That OK was good enough. That *I* was good enough. So I made these OK buttons. They say OK on one side and then on the other side they have affirmations, like You are beautiful, You are kind, You are generous, You are good. Then, for the ritual, I took my effigy up to a cliff. Everybody was gathered there with me and I told them what this ball represented to me. Then I took a baseball bat that I had named Tawanda [remember the movie *Fried Green Tomatoes*?] and I smashed that thing to smithereens and yelled and screamed at it. It split open—like a piñata—and the roses and the candy fell out. I said, 'Okay, come on everybody, get some goodies!' " She laughs.

"So Kwan Yin on my altar holds my OK button and reminds me. And she's holding one of the roses from the ritual, too. I think a big part of my healing is being gentle with myself, so in that sense Kwan Yin is helping me with my healing. She does teach me about compassion. She reminds me about it."

Showing me the items on the altar, she points out the lotus stem. "Marion Woodman talks about how our suffering becomes the source of our power and wisdom, the source of our compassion. And that is what the lotus is about, you know, that out of the mud comes this incredible beauty. But it needs the mud. That's real good for a perfectionist like me to remember."

So Marylou works with her Kwan Yin as a way of loosening and softening her internal judging and of having the best kind of life she can manage while living with lung cancer. "When I'm writing in my journal," she concludes, "I will sometimes thank her, sometimes ask her for help. She just feels a lot closer to me, and a lot more accepting, than my old God the Father."

Rite of Passage

One might wonder if the person chooses the tattoo or the tattoo chooses the person. Tattoo has been considered part of a rite of passage in many cultures as long as people have lived together. Once one bears the mark, one's life has changed forever.

Meghan Skye

To welcome Kwan Yin into one's consciousness is one thing; to etch her permanently into one's skin is quite another. Meghan Skye has made this "lifetime commitment" with a spectacular tattoo that covers most of her back.

This image does not look like the Chinese Kwan Yins with which most of us are familiar. Inspired by Japanese tattoo art, the female figure is drawn from Kabuki theater. Kabuki is a form of Japanese theater dating from the seventeenth century, with formalized pantomime, dance, and song. So Kwan Yin (who is called Kannon or Kanzeon in Japan) resembles a Japanese maiden with an elaborate hairdo, wearing a beautiful kimono. She stands on a huge golden carp, which, Meghan tells me, is how the goddess often appears in Japanese mythology. The carp represents stoicism, bravery, the willingness to see something through no matter what the price. Meghan elaborates: "In mythology, it is said that when a carp is hooked, it will not flap around or try to get away, but rather accepts its fate bravely." Maple leaves circle the figure of maiden and carp, some green, some brown, to symbolize the turning of the seasons, the passage of time. At the upper left of the tattoo are two Japanese characters that represent two people joining their *ki* (vital energy/spirit) to create something new and totally different from themselves (see figure 7).

On the deck of her small frame house near the Russian River, Meghan bares her back to show me the work of art that is a permanent part of her body. I am stunned by its grace and intricacy, the gold of the carp pooling and deepening the sunlight, the maiden resplendent in her flowing kimono blown by the sea wind.

Meghan was twenty-five years old when she designed the image herself, in collaboration with a tattoo artist, and endured many long agonizing hours of having it etched into her skin. Unlike most people, who do many very short sessions to accomplish a large tattoo, Meghan acquired her Kwan Yin in only a few five-to six-hour agonizing sessions. "I did it in a pretty

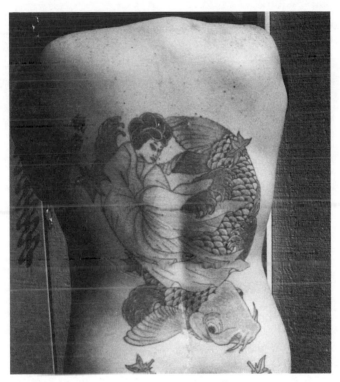

Figure 7. Meghan Skye's Kabuki Kwan Yin tattoo.

world-record kind of way," she says, smiling. She has taken me inside and we sit down to talk. This young woman with her short auburn hair and pleasant face looks as if she is strong and athletic, a deceptive impression.

In reality she is acquainted with extreme physical suffering, which helps explain why she would choose to wear the goddess of mercy on her back. Her father died when she was three years old. At the age of thirteen she was almost killed in a motorcycle accident. Both of her legs were crushed, causing her to spend a year in bed and undergo ten surgeries. Then, from a blood transfusion she contracted hepatitis C. "In saving my life," she says, "they gave me this terminal illness. It's chronic, but you die from it eventually." Then, at age twenty-one, because of liver complications, she had to have her gallbladder removed, and an extraordinary event occurred.

"It was a really dark time for me," Meghan says, "and I had what they call sometimes now a shamanic experience. What I experienced was three days of death, and then my life was new. In native culture they actually even sometimes bury the person, to represent the death of that old life and the new life that comes from it. It wasn't like being in a coma. It was a psychological experience of three days of death, and then a whole turnaround of everything. I came out of that knowing that my life was mostly dedicated to service to other people.

"And that is who Kwan Yin is. She's the goddess of mercy, she is the enlightened being who has *chosen*— unlike those wimps Buddha and Allah and Christ who, when they got spiritual enlightenment, were gone, you'll never hear from *them* again—Kwan Yin reaches enlightenment and chooses to stay on the wheel of life to help other people achieve spiritual enlightenment."

Meghan, who now at age thirty-five works part time managing a computer shop and studies literature at Sonoma State College, found Kwan Yin not through a Buddhist context but through tattoo. After her shamanic experience, as a student of psychology, she did a study of tattooing in different cultures. "I started studying the Japanese tattoo because that's where art in tattoo has really come in. Japanese tattoos are beautiful. The Japanese use symbols from their mythology and put them on their body to strengthen them, to assist them. A lot of firemen have water tattoos." She laughs. "Protection. If a man gets hurt and one shoulder is weaker, often he'll get a dragon tattooed on that shoulder, to strengthen him. Dragons symbolize the meeting of the yin and the yang: they're a fire entity that lives in water. The ultimate balance. And strength.

"So I was studying these symbols and mythology and came across Kwan Yin. I chose Kwan Yin because my life runs easier when I don't forget that my job is service. As long as I keep that in mind, everything runs along pretty well. As soon as I start to forget that and go on my own little trip and have my own little ego time, I get slammed. Something bad will happen to me. Inevitably.

"So I figured, what better reminder," she laughs, "than to have this huge thing on your back sort of as a totem. As a strengthener. And as a reminder."

Because the tattoo is on her back, she rarely sees it herself, except sometimes when getting out of the

shower she glimpses it in the mirror. She placed it
below her shoulders so that it would not be visible to
other people when she wears a tank top. The beautiful
image is not for show; it is her personal totem, symbol
of her rite of passage.

Meghan has worn the tattoo for ten years. In that
time she worked as a masseuse but had to stop when
serious back problems required surgery. (The scar from
this surgery is visible on the carp.) What does "being of
service" mean to her now? I ask.

She explains that because of her multiple physical
difficulties, she is now technically and actually disabled. Always before, even with the problems she had,
she had been very physically active, working out at a
gym, keeping her body in good shape. She does not
yet know how being severely physically limited will
change her life-path. In the meantime, she maintains
her commitment to serve.

"To be of service, it's so big. It's not so unusual for
me to run into a spirit, say, who is lost and needs a little
direction. That's being of service. Even just telling one
person, you know, one thing that is going to make their
life different. You can't measure that. It's how you come
in contact with people—with the intention to listen.
I don't think there are many people who are listened
to, who are really heard."

And I think of Kwan Yin, She Who Hears the Cries of
the World.

The Essence of Kwan Yin

One of my earliest encounters with Kwan Yin was a
book title that I kept seeing in the mid-eighties: *The*

Kwan Yin Book of Changes, by Diane Stein. I understood it to be a woman's version of the classical Chinese
book of divination, the *I Ching* or Book of Changes.
Stein took the very masculine *I Ching* and reworked it,
using the spiritual lore of many cultures in addition to
the Chinese, to respond to the needs and preoccupa-
tions of women (it was republished as *A Woman's
I Ching*).

This is only one of the many books published by
healer Diane Stein, who writes about Reiki bodywork,
natural healing, women's spirituality, and feminist
metaphysics. (Reiki is the art of applying universal life
energy—*ki*—to promote healing and wholeness.) She
has been active in the political areas of AIDS, incest
recovery, and disability rights. Her life is dedicated to
healing and to teaching women to heal themselves,
others, and the earth.

I wondered how Kwan Yin has figured in Diane
Stein's thirty years of service. From her home in Florida, Diane told me that the title of that early book was
chosen by her publisher and that the content of the
book itself had nothing to do with Kwan Yin. However,
the naming of the book may have been prophetic, for
soon after its publication she had a very strong encounter with Kwan Yin.

At the time she was living in Pittsburgh and was so
poor that she was homeless, subsisting on food stamps.
It was an extremely difficult period of her life. She
came to California to do a weekend training in Reiki,
which she was already practicing and teaching. At this
retreat, a woman gave her a porcelain statue of Kwan
Yin. Diane could tell that the statue was very old and
probably very valuable. She tried to refuse the gift,

afraid it might be broken on the airplane home, but the woman insisted she take it with her. So she carefully wrapped it up and brought it home to Pittsburgh. This Kwan Yin statue was the one valuable object that she owned.

From then on, Kwan Yin images began to come into her life, and her fortunes changed. Finding Kwan Yin, she says, "was a sign of hope to me. She's really all the goddesses together."

Now Diane Stein lives in Florida, where she owns her own house and has achieved a level of prosperity undreamed of in her poverty-stricken years. She continues to find and bring home Kwan Yin statues from antique stores and has about thirty of these images in her home. "My house is a temple to Kwan Yin," she tells me.

"And you know, her saving power is not just for human beings, it's for animals, too." Usually Diane does not kill any other beings, but roaches she cannot tolerate, and so she crushes them. She tells about a roach that escaped her and ran under one of the Kwan Yin statues. Laughing, she says, "When I lifted up the statue, I couldn't find it."

Now, besides her healing work and her writing, Diane has begun to use flowers and gemstones to create healing essences. She tells about a weekend when she was teaching Reiki in her own house. She had planted pink camellias in her garden but had been told that they would not thrive. She wanted to use them for her "Kwan Yin essence," which is an infusion of pink camellia and gemstones in water. During the workshop, a full moon rose, and the camellias bloomed. Diane hurried to make the essence. Some water remained in the bowl when she was finished, so she gave it to the workshop participants, who drank it. "After that," she says, "they were seeing Kwan Yin all evening in the house."

Diane describes herself as "partially a Buddhist, mostly a witch," and she is certainly a mystic. Her most recent book, *We Are the Angels,* gives directions for "healing our past, present, and future" with entities that she calls the Lords of Karma. Her work is strongly promoted in *The Essential Reiki Journal,* published by Robyn C. Zimmerman in Maryland (see Books and Articles). It is from Zimmerman's organization, Essential Healing Circle, Inc., that the Kwan Yin flower and gemstone essences are available. In the *Journal* the Kwan Yin Essence is described as derived from pink camellia and the gemstones kunzite, pink morganite, aquamarine, danburite, and clear quartz crystal. Each essence is prepared by Diane Stein with flowers from her garden and gemstones from her personal collection. According to Robyn Zimmerman, "Diane follows a sacred procedure that honors the Goddess and the Deva of each plant." She meditates, and in that state she requests the permission of the plant to become part of the essence and asks for its willingness to participate in healing. "The essences are infused with Reiki energy while they are being distilled and again before they are bottled," Robyn explains. "Overseeing the entire operation is the Celtic Goddess Brede, or Bridgit. She tells Diane which gemstones to select and describes the attributes of each essence." The Kwan Yin Essence benefits the heart chakra, "bringing healing and compassion into one's life; [it] encourages forgiveness, inner peace,

self-esteem, calm certainty, heart healing; aids meditation, promotes love of Goddess and Universal love."

Diane treasures a two-foot-high Kwan Yin statue
brought to her from Thailand. Carved of dark wood, the
female figure holds a snake in her hand. The snake curls
down to form the base of the statue. In Thailand, Diane
tells me, Kwan Yin is known as Gom Lin.

And for all of her more esoteric work in healing
energy bodies and selves, clearing karma and undoing
karmic damage (which is her most recent effort in workshops and in her writing), and her very broad understanding of spirituality, Diane Stein always returns to
Kwan Yin energy, which she sees as compassion, comfort, mercy. Because, as she says, "You go to her when
you're hurting."

Kwan Yin as Comforter and Healer

One might ask, why would lesbian women want to
meet separately to practice Buddhist meditation? Why
couldn't they have the same experience in a heterosexual meditation community? The women of the Berkeley
Lesbian Sangha (*sangha* means, loosely, "community")
might answer that in a heterosexual environment they
tend to disappear. If the leader is giving a "Dharma
talk" on relationships, invariably it is male–female relations that are referred to. The assumptions made about
how people live always correspond to a heterosexual
lifestyle, and so the lesbian woman begins to feel invisi-
ble, unacknowledged, dismissed.

Carol Newhouse, responding to these conditions, has
provided a context in which lesbians meet regularly to

pursue their meditation and hear speakers on Buddhist subjects. As the leader of the Lesbian Sangha, she relies strongly on her relationship with Kwan Yin.

"When I formed the Berkeley Lesbian Sangha, I knew one of my central motivations was to bring Kwan Yin into the lives of women, especially lesbians, to make her more accessible to us. Much of what has always concerned me about my community of women friends, and especially lesbians, is our resistance to kindness and compassion, especially as expressed toward ourselves.

"I have come to understand this tendency as a natural response in an oppressed group. Prejudice and discrimination are directed at us, and sometimes we take that and internalize it and apply it to ourselves in a self-rejecting way, as well as projecting it out onto others. Often we end up living in a struggle rather than living in the space that Kwan Yin provides, where you dwell in the mind and heart of kindness."

Lesbians need sanctuary from this struggle, the safety to open to spirituality and practice. Carol sees Kwan Yin as helping to create this space of refuge by her very nature, by being available to receive communication and requests for help. She can represent the unconditionally loving mother that many people have never known.

"Kwan Yin helps us heal our tendency toward constriction and self-criticism, by helping us open our hearts. At our Sangha meetings our sessions often end with an appreciation meditation. I invoke Kwan Yin at those moments, asking that we open to ourselves and to each other in gratitude and appreciation of the beauty and radiance of who we really are. I can truly feel her presence then, it's as if the air is filled with her understanding and love."

An image of Kwan Yin that is popular with Lesbian Sangha women shows her sitting in meditation with one foot out ahead of her on the floor. That posture signals that she is ready to move to action in the service of healing and the alleviation of suffering. This appeals to many women because they find the service aspect important to their Buddhist practice. "In this posture," says Carol, "Kwan Yin becomes more of a modern goddess, not so passive, more action-oriented."

On her own altar at home Carol has a statue of Kwan Yin as the many-armed goddess. In her numerous hands, Kwan Yin holds various objects: money, pens, sacred texts, flowers, food, rising and setting suns, all instruments to use in aiding other creatures (see figure 8). "For me," Carol explains, "she embodies a multitude of expressions of a bodhisattva of which I might be capable. She broadens my understanding of the myriad ways kindness and compassion might express themselves through me. She is a real inspiration to my practice of Buddhism in daily life. But also in the context of community. In this Kwan Yin I see each of us expressing kindness as best we know how, and in whatever way we can. Sometimes sitting in meditation in front of the Sangha, I open my eyes and look upon the faces of the women present, and I can see Kwan Yin in each expression, and Kwan Yin's love expressed through each life.

"I would like to think that when I die, I will have developed the wisdom and courage so that at the moment of passing I can step over the threshold into her loving embrace."

Figure 8. Many-Armed Kwan Yin bought in Oakland
Chinatown. (Photo by Carol Newhouse.)

The Kwan Yin Revolutionary Army

In the gentle wooded hills of Mill Valley, in a multi-level house full of light and color, live bodyworker Elaine Belle and musician Sheilah Glover with their new baby, Zena Lotus Belle Glover, whom they adopted from a Chinese orphanage.

Elaine holds Zena on her lap as we talk in the baby room, strewn with toys for the eighteen-month-old. Elaine, a dark-haired, gentle woman, has experienced a strong connection with Kwan Yin since someone gave her John Blofeld's *Bodhisattva of Compassion* in the mid-seventies. After reading the book, she began to do meditations visualizing Kwan Yin. She then had a piercing experience.

"A little girl named Cary lived next door. I'd gotten really close to this child. She was only about five, and she used to come over and hang out with me a lot—a great kid. Then she got leukemia, and for a while she was really ill, it seemed clear that she was dying. I used to go to be with her at the hospital. I would send Kwan Yin to her when I was meditating and try to bring some calmness there. Then when she went home to die, I could feel there was a lot of turmoil in her house. So at one point I went and just sat down in my room—I really had no idea what was going on with her—and I did this long meditation where I saw Kwan Yin scooping her up and holding her. It felt so clear, I could see her really being with Cary. And then I found out the next day that Cary had died exactly at the time I was sitting in meditation.

"So that was the first real strong impact. Then after

that whenever I was in trouble or had problems, I could just remember Kwan Yin and it was like a real presence would come. It made much more sense to me than anything else I had done in terms of religion. The meditations I did with Kwan Yin I could feel in my bones and my heart. The very innermost part of my body would just sort of vibrate and get wide. It was wonderful to have that connection."

Zena Lotus has offered me her bottle and patted my hand; now she is tired. Elaine takes her into another room to put her down for a nap. When she returns, we talk about how Kwan Yin helped Elaine reconnect with her mother.

Elaine's mother, a working woman all her life, entertains herself by going to antique stores and yard sales to buy and collect things. She has become expert in assessing the value and history of the objects she buys. Elaine's sister is able to join her mother in these outings, but it is not an activity that interests Elaine.

In fact, Elaine confided that she and her mother have never been very close. "She told my younger sister one day, 'You know, I just don't understand Elaine.' But somehow she—well, I had had a Kwan Yin when I was in high school. I'd gone to San Francisco Chinatown with an aunt and for some reason I really wanted this statue—I didn't even know it was Kwan Yin at the time—and bought it. I knew nothing about her and never learned anything until much later when someone gave me that book [Bodhisattva of Compassion].

"Then about four years ago my mother was cleaning out stuff, and she found that statue with some of my

things from high school, so she sent the Kwan Yin
statue to me. I thanked her and told her I appreciated it.
And then for some reason, something clicked, and she
realized, 'Oh, Elaine likes Kwan Yins, maybe I'll collect
those.' So one day she sent me a box and there must
have been at least fifteen of them in there. As she went
her rounds of the sales, every time she would see one
she'd buy it. She had this great little supply, and she
sent them to me.

"It was such a gesture of acceptance and love, it just
filled me with delight. I thought, 'Of course, how wonderful!' And it reactivated that connection and got me
thinking about Kwan Yin. My mother, of course, wasn't
relating to it in a spiritual way, she was just collecting,
you know, thinking, 'This would be something that
Elaine would like.' It was her finding some way to let me
know that there is a connection between us, that she
does love me. She's really trying to understand me.
I talked to her a little bit about Kwan Yin and compared
her to Mary because I thought that was something she
could relate to."

Elaine takes me into the living room to see the collection of small white ceramic Kwan Yins her mother sent
her, arranged on a shelf with a branch of flowering
lemon tree.

We return to the couch, and she tells me about her
work. Elaine does Alexander bodywork, a process of
"movement education" exploring how one's body
alignment affects one's posture and movement pat-
terns. For performers, who need precision in body
movement, and for people who have been injured in
accidents and are experiencing pain, the technique

helps to find the core of the body and expand the range of movement. Sometimes in her work she uses meditation, and sometimes with specific clients she calls in Kwan Yin. With a recent client, who has since died, she had a particularly affirming experience.

"When she first came to me," Elaine says, looking rueful, "she was just so resentful and angry and complaining about everything. I thought, 'Oh, how am I going to work with this person?' She had cancer. I gave her some suggestions of things to do. I didn't mention Kwan Yin the first session. She came back the next session, and she had followed my suggestions. She was a changed person. I was so impressed with her ability to change. And then after that, at different times we would do prayers for her and it always would start with calling in Kwan Yin and feeling that. And there was a Kwan Yin meditation that I had her do. A lot of times these things would just come to me to do with her, and I couldn't repeat them to you now. She would talk about them the next time and I had trouble remembering exactly what I had said to her. But it really helped *her* a lot.

"She ended up eventually meditating at a local Buddhist center and the *metta* [loving kindness] meditation was her focus after a while, really working with compassion for herself and others. Right before she died of cancer, she had these really sweet experiences. She lived in a duplex, and this guy lived right next door. They had started out kind of friendly but then something went wrong, and so for years they'd been at odds with each other. He would blast his music and upset her, and she really tried to make amends, but he just kept being this constant irritating force; she couldn't even garden in the backyard because he was there. She told me that the cancer was very healing because it got her in touch with how much she needed to take care of herself and have compassion for herself. So she met this guy on the street, and she stopped and said, 'John, I just want to tell you I'm sorry for any problems I've ever caused you. I meant no harm.' Then he kind of broke down and said, 'I'm really sorry, too'—I mean, they had been warring with each other for four or five years—and they hugged in the street. It was just amazing. And there were other stories like that with people that she'd really been at odds with: she ran into them and would say she was sorry for any harm she had caused them and that she wanted to make amends. It was just amazing. I always thought it had to do with Kwan Yin, 'cause we really did work with the compassion and opening the heart.

"As for me, it feels that Kwan Yin comes at different times when I really need her. It's like I can feel that presence. And then I'll have long periods when I don't think about her. I'm sure talking about her now is going to just bring her in. And I think Zena's going to have a connection with her."

Sheilah Glover has joined us now, and we talk about their new daughter. Sheilah is a tall woman with a performer's bright, light-filled presence, quick and with more of an edge to her than Elaine. She shows me a painting of the "Red Thread Kwan Yin," which depicts a Kwan Yin pouring sacred fluid down upon a baby enclosed in a nimbus and trailing a red thread. The belief is, Sheilah tells me, that each baby is connected to its true parents by a thread, and she and Elaine feel that they have this connection with Zena, even though they had to go halfway around the globe to find her. (This very female-looking Kwan Yin has a small mustache and may represent a transitional figure between the male Avalokitesvara and the fully female Kwan Yin; see figure 9.)

There was a moment when Elaine had her doubts about adopting a baby from a culture so different from her own, but then she looked around and remembered her strong connection to Kwan Yin, her practice of *Chi Gung* (a Chinese form of body movement), her use of acupuncture as a healing modality. Sheilah's connection to China came through art and literature. Years ago when she saw some Chinese landscape paintings, she fell in love with them. And the work of Chinese poets became important to her.

They tell about their trip to Canton to pick up Zena. They were guided by a Chinese man from Los Angeles who goes every three weeks or so to China with twelve to fifteen families, matches them to female babies in orphanages, and brings them back. He is only one of the agents who connect American families with Chinese babies. The plight of Chinese girl babies is well known. In China, where each family is allowed only one child, it is almost always a boy baby who is desired, as funeral ceremonies must be performed by a man, and a man will be better able to provide for his aged parents than a woman, who must go to live in her husband's family. So thousands of girl babies are abandoned in places where they will be found and put in orphanages.

Figure 9. "Red Thread Kwan Yin" with mustache.

Elaine explained to me that she and Sheilah will never know the birth mother of Zena, for it is illegal in China to abandon a child, and so the parents maintain strict secrecy. The fees paid by foreigners adopting these little Chinese girls help to maintain the system of state orphanages in which some of them spend years waiting to be adopted.

Sheilah tells me that there are now 8,500 newly adopted Chinese girls in the United States and the number is constantly growing. A thousand New York City families adopted Chinese babies last year, and many of these families were Jewish, so the babies are breaking a number of cultural boundaries.

Zena Lotus is an extraordinary little girl. On Elaine's lap, she sat with her ankles crossed, like a little Kwan Yin, watching me, and gave the impression of great will and determination. As well, there is a sweetness to her, as she leaned toward me offering me her bottle to drink from.

Sheilah laughs, telling an idea that intrigues her. "While we were on the trip to China, this woman Virginia had this same fantasy as did another woman—we all had this collective idea that these girls are going to turn out to be revolutionaries and go back to China and kick butt. You know, support the Dalai Lama and free Tibet. I wanted someone to write a book about it, all these twenty-five-year-old girls meeting in some Mission Street apartment in San Francisco, you know, they've all grown up here, disenfranchised from their homeland, and just bright as whips 'cause they've had every possible upper-middle-class advantage, and, you

know, they're organizing. It's the Kwan Yin Revolutionary Army!"

Elaine smiles gently. "Zena has a great little picture
of Kwan Yin hanging in her crib, and she likes to play
with it every now and then."

Sheilah nods. "Right. This is one baby who will definitely grow up knowing who Kwan Yin is."

Give Me a Hand, Kwan Yin

The White-Robed Kwan Yin—the representation that most
resembles the Virgin Mary—is known for her ability to con-
fer children upon those who ask for them. Some of the
small white ceramic statues of the White-Robed Kwan
Yin have a detachable hand that can be pulled out of the
sleeve of her robe.

The belief is that when you want something, you petition Kwan Yin. Then you take the small white hand and
hide it somewhere in your house. Kwan Yin, presumably,
is so distressed at losing her hand that she will grant you
your wish. Then when your desire has been granted, you
find the little hand and replace it on the statue.

Gwendolyn, an acquaintance of mine, desperately
wanted to give birth to a baby but was unable to conceive.
She heard about the Kwan Yin myth, bought a statue, and
hid the hand. In the following year she became pregnant.
Now the proud mother of a child, she searches in vain for
the white ceramic hand. Perhaps when the baby becomes
a toddler, curious about all the secret places in the house,
she will find the hand herself.

This myth may come loosely from a story about the
White-Robed Kwan Yin's arrival on Chinese shores. In the
eleventh century, it is said, Kwan Yin came over the ocean
to the city of Chiang-yin. She was sighted by a passenger

on a ship, who saw her among the waves, a white-robed figure following the boat, her body swathed in bright light. Head up, toes barely grazing the water, snowy robe flowing out behind her, she sailed forward in a brilliant aureole. Disturbed by this apparition, the boatman pushed at her with his pole, but she kept on coming and the light never dimmed. Giving up on the boat, she finally sailed into the mouth of the river to rest.

That night she visited a townsman in a dream and asked him to provide her with a right arm. When he pleaded that he could not part with his arm, she said there was a piece of sandalwood in a shop in the town, and he could use it to fashion an arm. At daybreak, the man heard a report that a ten-foot-high statue of Kwan Yin had been found at the riverbank. Hurrying to take a look, he saw that the statue was missing its right arm, and he understood the significance of his dream. He obtained the piece of sandalwood from the shop and created an arm for the statue. The townspeople took the image and put it in their temple. Perhaps in gratitude for her new arm, Kwan Yin always responded to their prayers. (From Chün-fang Yü)

Battling the Dogs of Hell

Terri Nicholson was one of the early American students of Master Hua, the Chinese Buddhist teacher who founded a number of monasteries on American soil. She lives with her family in an old wooden house on the grounds of the City of Ten Thousand Buddhas, the institution located near Ukiah in Northern California. Terri welcomes me into her living room and agrees to tell me about her relationship with Kwan Yin, if I make it clear that she does not speak for the monastery but only for herself as a private person.

We sit in her pleasant living room, furnished in modest beige. Terri, dressed in a casual sweater and jeans, has long straight dark graying hair; her eyes are friendly behind glasses. While a young student of Chinese and religious studies, she lived with the nuns and was drawn to their lifestyle, but she did not take the robes because she knew that her life was with family and children. For many years she worked in the school at City, both as teacher and director. She is married and has two children of her own. Her husband is a carpenter and woodworker who did much of the work in the Buddha Hall.

After describing her early involvement with Master Hua, which came about through her brother, and her many years of commitment ("I have been a Buddhist for more than twenty years. I took refuge with the Master in 1973."), she tells me about an experience with Kwan Yin.

When Terri's daughter was three years old, the family went to Mount Lassen for a visit with her husband's brother. It was a very mixed experience from the beginning. "We were not comfortable there. The first place we were staying had a stream where people could pick out their fish for dinner (followers of Master Hua are strict vegetarians) and they had penned baby deer whose parents had been killed. We ended up staying outside the park because we were so uncomfortable. But we did spend a couple of days hiking around the park and my daughter had a frightening experience in one of the caves. Marcelle was on her uncle's shoulders, and got very, very frightened, and talked constantly after that moment about wanting to go home to see Master Hua. When we got back here, she started having

nightmares—in the dreams she was being bitten by
dogs—wolves, she said. I didn't pay that much attention—told her to recite Kwan Yin's name. Then several
months later she began to wake up in the morning
screaming that her legs hurt."

Terri and her husband took their daughter to doctors,
who could not find anything wrong. They put the child
on antibiotics, and she had an allergic reaction. "Then
it got to the point where she couldn't walk! And she
would wake up screaming in pain."

When they took Marcelle to see Master Hua, he
looked at her and said, "The doctors are not going to
find anything."

Still hoping for help from Western medicine, Terri
consulted an orthopedist and a pediatrician, who specu-
lated that a virus might be causing the pain and swell-
ing in her daughter's legs.

"The Master kept asking, 'Where have you taken her?
Where did you go with her?' We wracked our brains,
and we finally remembered the Mount Lassen trip.
When we made the connection, I called the Master and
told him, and he said, 'Why would you go somewhere
where there is a volcano? You Americans don't understand anything.' He explained to us that a place like
that is like hell on earth, and the beings that hang out
there are hell beings. (I remembered that the names of
the places there were things like Bumpass Hell—they
were boiling mud pots.) He said that some of the creatures that lived there in spirit form were fire-breathing
dogs. They're actually spoken of in the sutras. And that
because Marcelle was so pure and so young, and having
grown up here in the monastery, that they were very

attracted to her, fell in love with her, and wanted her to become part of their retinue. So they were biting her, and that's what all of the pain was!

"You can imagine how I felt. I was just devastated that I hadn't known and had taken her to this place. She was close to death at this point. I could tell. She was losing control over her bodily functions, and she was just in horrible pain. The only way that she would stop crying was if we could get her to recite to Kwan Yin.

"At that point I talked to the Master and he said to me, 'Don't let her get angry.' Although she was normally sweet-natured, during this illness she had a huge temper. But she was a very verbal three-year-old, so we made all these charts, you know, star charts. And she said to me at that point, 'Put no growling on the chart.' (This was before he had told me anything about the dogs.)

"So we worked with her, and when she would recite she'd fall asleep. I also had a tape of the Master reciting the Earth Treasure Bodhisattva's name, and when I played that she would fall asleep. But every time she'd wake up, she would be screaming in pain.

"The Master said, 'You have to be more sincere.' He was really fierce, he was not at all reassuring, which was not like him. 'You have to be more sincere.' We recited the Great Compassion Mantra and Kwan Yin's name constantly. We would chant in the house, and then my husband and I would go up to the Buddha Hall and bow the Great Compassion Repentance every day.

"The Master came to our house and sat with Marcelle. And every time she asked for him, he came immediately, which he didn't normally do. He would just come and sit with her for a little while. And she very gradually got better.

"The pain went away. She couldn't walk for a long time. But the Master said, 'Don't worry, she'll be okay.' We did a meal offering when she was a lot better, made a meal and offered it to the Triple Jewel [the Buddha, Dharma, and Sangha], and by the end of the meal she was running around with the other kids.

"It was a very long process, about six months. I feel very, very clear that if it wasn't for Kwan Yin Bodhisattva and the Master, my daughter would have died. [Her daughter is now a healthy sixteen-year-old.] I'm a very concrete person, I'm not a person who sees visions or any of that kind of thing. But it was a real lesson for me about the world beyond what we see. *I* had dreams of these dogs. They were huge with big teeth, very frightening."

Terri feels that her whole life has been blessed by Kwan Yin Bodhisattva. "Everything about my life has been amazingly smooth, more than most people." One of the things that most moves her, she says, is the all-accepting compassion of Kwan Yin.

"To me, that's the most important thing in Buddhism, that there's no one who does not have the Buddha nature, and so compassion reaches out to those who are doing evil as well as those who are doing good. It's not that we change who we are, but we transform what's already there. To me, that's one of the most wonderful things. You're never put outside where there's no hope. You can't get outside the Dharma Realm. It may be many eons before you're ready to listen, but there's never any forsaking of anybody. There's a deep comfort in that.

"We all have Kwan Yin in us. It's come to me over the years that we all suffer from loneliness, that's probably our deepest affliction, and what loneliness is, is not realizing our connections with all other beings. We feel separate, we feel different. Enlightenment is understanding the connection, that we aren't separate.

"So we cultivate the practice with Kwan Yin Bodhisattva, hoping to learn to be like her and have the deep compassion that connects us with all living beings."

The Mount Shasta Communications

Thinking about Kwan Yin, I remembered hearing that a woman I knew had made pilgrimages to the spectacular snowy slopes of Mount Shasta in Northern California to contact Kwan Yin. Gina Covina, a painter, novelist, and publisher, for some years had run an artists' retreat in Vallecitos, New Mexico.

When I called about this project, Gina said she would be happy to talk to me about her Mount Shasta experience. It had been so long since she had even thought of it, she said, and it might be interesting to revisit it. I found Gina in an adobe house in Vallecitos. Her big, bear-like dog Baya came out to greet me, and Gina and I went inside to talk.

It was 1982 or 1983, Gina tells me as we settle on a couch, when she was living in Berkeley, that she heard from her friend named Juana, who was engaged in intensive meditation. Juana told her that she kept feeling some entity wanting to speak through her. Juana was terrified by that prospect.

"So I said, 'Why don't you have me be there, and I'll ground for you and ask it what it wants. We'll see what's happening and it won't be too scary.' So she had me come over, and she meditated, and this entity—who knows what *that* is—this *thing* began to speak through her and said it was a group of beings focused at Mount Shasta. They had come into the mountain as their re-entry onto the planet, they said, and then from there they were going to disperse. One of them was Kwan Yin, and one was the Virgin Mary."

"Re-entry from where?" I ask.

Gina blinks. "I don't know. I think by re-entry they meant they were just making themselves more available. As we listened, sometimes there would be messages from the whole group, and sometimes there would be messages from Kwan Yin alone. Juana would identify which it was. Juana did that channeling. I also did channeling then, but I wrote it down, just automatic writing, not looking at the page."

Gina gazes intently at me. "The thing that interested me a lot was that Kwan Yin and the Virgin Mary had forged some new relationship that was bridging East and West. Because they together are the mothers of the world, they were consciously taking on that role in some united way. That's the sense I got. It wasn't that I was putting them together—they had somehow taken on this new way of being in relation to each other, in order to do what was needed in the world for this time."

The beings said they were based in Mount Shasta, and they invited Gina and Juana to come visit. So Gina found a survey map of Mount Shasta, and the next time Juana sat down to channel, Gina unrolled the map and asked, "Okay, where are you?"

Juana raised her finger in the air and brought it down on the map, and they marked an X where she had put her finger. It was a spot on the side of the mountain, near a little spring, several miles from a road. The place was up quite high, it appeared, around tree line on the south side of the mountain, with nothing around it.

As it was the middle of winter, Gina and Juana did not make a trip up north to Mount Shasta. That next summer, Gina and another friend were on a driving trip to Colorado from California and they came back the northern route. Suddenly, there they were, driving down Route 5 past Mount Shasta. They did not have the map with them, but they remembered something of where the spot was. They decided to stop in at the Forest Service office to see if the rangers had a map and whether they could recognize it that way.

"So we stopped in," Gina tells me, "and they not only had a map but they had a *photocopied map* of the exact spot that we were looking for! It had a name, which I can't remember now. But it was a spring, and there was a trail that went most of the way to it, and then it was possible to walk across the scree to this spring. It was in the afternoon; we didn't have a lot of daylight, but we figured we had time to go there. So we drove to the end of the road and then, following the map, we walked up the mountain and came to a beautiful timberline spring where the water came out from under the glacier, and there were low pines around and big rocks. We sat there for a little while, and the energy was very intense."

Later, looking for information on Mount Shasta, Gina found the account of a man named Guy Ballard, who was a surveyor on the mountain in the 1920s. He had camped out at that spring and had an encounter with a mountain lion there; then he was visited by St. Germain, who was one of the beings in the group that Juana was channeling. St. Germain showed him a cave in the side of the mountain. Guy Ballard wrote about his encounter, and he went on to start a religious organization, called the I Am Foundation, which maintains a temple in Oakland.

Meanwhile, Juana had gone to see a very old woman in Sausalito who was a psychic teacher. She wanted to have some other opinion of this channeling she was doing, so she sent the woman the transcripts of what she'd been receiving and then went to meet her. Gina opens her eyes wide. "And this woman said, 'Oh yeah, we all know about this. She gave Juana the date in the 1980s that these beings had entered the mountain and said a lot of people saw it, there was this big cone of light that went down into Mount Shasta."

Other beings besides Kwan Yin who arrived included Thomas Jefferson and George Washington; Nikola Tesla (Tesla, who lived from 1856 to 1943, was an electrician and inventor who made discoveries in radio transmission and electricity; he designed the great power system at Niagara); St. Germain; and the Virgin Mary. Gina shrugs. "Who knows what happened? I don't know how that works—some were historical figures, some figures from universal myths.

"We went back a number of times. The place had incredible energy and intensity to it. It felt like some kind of initiation *just being there*. It was really a big power spot. So we would just go and be there."

When I ask if she did practices to Kwan Yin in her home, she says she and her partner had several images of Kwan Yin in the house. "One thing that was conveyed through the channeling was that her colors were a gold light, a rose light, and a lavender light. And we were instructed to meditate on and bathe our auras in those colors. So we had those colors around."

Does Gina have any of the communications she channeled during that time? I ask. She tells me it's quite extraordinary, but she does. She had put the papers into a file folder many years ago and put it away, but just yesterday, before I came, she found the folder. Now she brings it out and shows me the papers. Each segment of a few lines was written at the bottom of a page of drawing paper, as if she had intended to make a drawing for each.

"Use them," Gina says and hands me the folder.

And I have been using them since, putting them in various places in my house, reading them just before I go out the door or when I need help. And I have contemplated them in meditation. You will find many of these utterances in Chapter Four of this book, for you to use in this way.

The following is just one, which will give a sense of the content and feeling of these communications.

We are all indeed in the Great Transformation now.
  Do not be surprised at any appearance.

The two worlds are moving back together—their congruence is not complete, but close enough for dreams and waking to mingle and partake of the same events.

Use all your strength to love all that appears—in your inner being, in those persons around you, in the large world. That is the task.

Kwan Yin/The Prostitute

on her day off
the prostitute wakes up alone—
the night's chill

> Chiyo-ni (eighteenth-century
> woman haiku master of Japan)

In my travels I had met Buddhist poet Pat Donegan, who not only writes haiku and other kinds of poetry but co-translates the work of Asian women poets. She had been a strong practitioner of Tibetan Buddhism at Vajradhatu in Boulder and had taught poetry at the Naropa Institute there. I knew that she was very interested in and engaged with the figure of Kwan Yin.

But imagine my surprise several years ago when I was shown a poem written by Pat Donegan that associates Kwan Yin with a prostitute. Nowhere before had I seen Kwan Yin portrayed in a sexual context, and initially I felt that the juxtaposition was forced.

Kuan Yin/The Prostitute

She is passion and no passion
she is not separate from me
a projection of energy

of form, of emptiness
movements of things
may or may not exist

I am Kuan Yin/the prostitute
breathing together one breath
a whirling Shiva within the space of mind
imprints of a bird in sky
Kuan Yin/the prostitute different
yet the same

Love the prostitute in me
as well as Kuan Yin
darkness as well as light
Kuan Yin holds her arms
around the prostitute
the prostitute holds her arms
around Kuan Yin

Kuan Yin's lips bright red
no lips at all
prostitute/Kuan Yin did it to me
it was done
the opening,
lipstick on the wind, bright red.

This poem juxtaposes a prostitute with Kwan Yin to evoke a moment of heightened consciousness. Donegan sees that the seeming opposites of prostitute and virginal bodhisattva are one and that she has become united with them, destroying all duality and entering the emptiness—"lipstick on the wind"—through what she calls "the opening."

So I understood the poem on later reading, but my first reaction spurred me to delve more deeply into Kwan Yin lore. There I found several evocations of her that involve actual seduction and even promiscuous sex. As I mentioned, Kwan Yin came into Chinese culture through the personalities of supposedly historical women memorialized in folk tales, popular novels, and plays, as well as Buddhist texts. In the writings of scholar Chün-fang Yü I discovered that among Kwan Yin's several Chinese manifestations, there was a person called the Woman of Yen-chou, who was known to have "engaged in sexual activities in order to carry out the mission of salvation."

The Woman of Yen-chou

The Woman of Yen-chou lived in the late eighth century. "She had sex with any man who asked for it," writes Yü. "But whoever had sex with her was said to be free from sexual desire forever." However, the people of her village saw her simply as a dissolute woman of ill-repute. When she died at the age of twenty-four, she "was buried without ceremony in a common grave by the roadside." Later, a foreign monk paid respect at her grave. He told the villagers that the Woman of Yen-chou had acted out of compassion and that her bones were connected with golden chains, one of the signs of a holy person. When the villagers dug up her skeleton, they indeed found her bones linked by gold chains, and they recognized her as a sacred being. Later, through elaboration in myth and story, her identity as Kwan Yin was established.

Similar stories concern Mr. Ma's Wife or Kwan Yin with the Fish Basket; in these two manifestations, the woman was young and beautiful. She arrived in a province where the people had no interest in Buddhism, and she offered to marry the man who could memorize certain specified Buddhist scriptures in a short time. After several trials, Mr. Ma won out. But on the day of the wedding, before the union was consummated, Mr. Ma's wife died. After her burial, an old monk arrived and disinterred the bones, which were connected with a gold chain. "The monk told the assembled onlookers that the woman was a manifestation of a great sage who came in order to save them from their evil karma," and many people living in the region were converted to Buddhism.

Through the centuries, as this story was told and retold, Mr. Ma's wife became the bodhisattva Kwan Yin. She was also called Kwan Yin with the Fish Basket, for she was said to have arrived on Golden Sand Beach "as a fish-monger, carrying a basket of fish on her arm." Mr. Ma's wife was "eulogized as a skillful tamer of men. Using her dazzling beauty as bait, she frees people from the ocean of lust. Her trickery . . . was no more than using poison to counteract poison. . . . She first offered sexual favor, but then denied its gratification. She used sexual desire as a skillful means, a teaching device to help people to reach goodness."

In the scriptures of Mahayana Buddhism, the technique of using erotic desire as a goad to awakening is well documented. Yü points out that "sexuality, either offered outright or first promised and then later withheld, can serve as a powerful tool of spiritual transformation."

It is interesting to note that the story of the Woman of Yen-chou, who actually engaged in sexual relations, has been dropped from the accounts of Kwan Yin, while

Mr. Ma's wife and Kwan Yin with the Fish Basket, who kept their virginity while offering sex, remain. As the acceptance of sensual or sexual practices in tantric Buddhism declined in China during the tenth century, and as the puritanical influence of Neo-Confucianism grew stronger, the story of the Woman of Yen-chou, "with its explicit mention of sex and the unconventional transposition of values (prostitute = bodhisattva) proved to be too shocking for general consumption" (Yü).

Pat Donegan speaks of her own spiritual relationship to Kwan Yin as "almost a secret, almost imperceptible, like the scent of wafting incense or the fragrance of flowers from a distance—yet I have carried her scent with me these last thirty years."

Pat now lives in Japan after a Fulbright grant, where she has co-translated a book of poems by Japan's most famous woman haiku poet. The book, *Chiyo-ni Woman Haiku Master* (done with Yoshie Ishibashi), was published in 1998 (see Books and Articles). Pat's communication to me from Japan ended, "So, gratefully I will carry the scent of Kuan Yin with me my whole life, and hopefully something of her fragrance will waft to others as well—for she is a reminder of compassion, bidding us to soften and open on the spot—and the grace is to know that sometimes we can do it and sometimes we can't, but there is always that fresh new moment. As in Chiyo-ni's haiku,

> rouged lips
> forgotten—
> clear spring water,

when one forgets the self and opens to what is there—
then one can taste, smell, and see."

"A Kwan Yin Pagan Goddess Mass"

During my cancer surgery and the chemotherapy treatments that went on for twenty-five weeks, I listened
daily to a piece of music that deeply comforted me. Enti-
tled "She Carries Me," it is a chant, multilayered and
rich with voice and instrumental elements, yet simple
enough to follow easily; it was composed, performed,
and produced by singer/songwriter Jennifer Berezan.

Jennifer's association with Kwan Yin integrates her
participation in the Women's Spirituality movement,
her Buddhist meditation practice, and her political
activism. To Jennifer, Kwan Yin through her service to
others proves that "you can be a Buddhist and be politically active." And while she is familiar with many goddesses from a number of traditions, she has always
responded strongly to Kwan Yin.

"She has that female savioress energy," Jennifer
explains. "Maybe it's because of my connections to
Catholicism and Mary, I'm not sure, but she's able to
hold a kind of mother-goddess energy for me as well.
So it's not only that awareness which I can have with
Buddhism of what I do that causes me to suffer, but
there's a compassionate sort of nurturing, self-loving,
forgiving quality that she has. So I can have that awareness and also forgive myself and feel nurtured and
held."

The chant "She Carries Me" began as a phrase in Jennifer's head when she was jogging one evening in the

dark. She heard the words "She who hears the cries of the world" in her mind, and immediately she knew that she wanted to put this into a musical piece. Several years passed while she came back again and again to this concept, trying different ways to accomplish the piece.

We talk in her living room, Jennifer, with her dark hair and brilliant blue eyes, gesturing freely as she speaks.

"It started with that phrase and the idea of Kwan Yin. And then I heard my Catholic roots and the Hail Mary, which seemed in some ways similar. The calling on a female deity, a savior. But I couldn't use the Hail Mary as is. I wanted a truer description of Mary, as the creator of all things. So I rewrote the Hail Mary and I called it the Holy Mother. I wanted it done as vespers. I could hear the nuns in the convents whispering the Hail Mary throughout the night for hours and hours in their vespers, and I wanted them to be saying 'Holy Mother,' so I changed the words to

Holy Mother full of grace, power is with thee
Blessed are you, Queen of the universe, and blessed is all
    of creation
Holy Mother, maker of all things
Be with us now and always. Blessed Be.

"So there's the strong Kwan Yin melody that carries the line 'She who hears the cries of the world,' and then behind it you hear spoken these 'Holy Mother' vespers. That's a second layer.

"Then another layer was the real pagan, women's

spirituality, Wiccan, nature side to it. Mother Goddess energy. I had Olympia Dukakis reciting 'The Charge of the Goddess,' a text based on a traditional piece by a woman in England, adapted by Doreen Valiente and Starhawk."

Jennifer tells how, in putting together the chant, "There's a part that whispers quietly, very subliminal, and it's based on something in the Catholic Church called 'the prayers of the faithful,' where at a certain time during the mass there are prayers that are made for various things, people's situations in the world. There are these prayers of the faithful that are being whispered underneath the other voices and the music— prayers for those who have AIDS, for those in prison, there's a whole litany of concerns and prayers that are voiced throughout."

One side of the tape ends with a song, "She Carries Me" (see Chapter Four), and the other side ends with a violin rendering of this song.

The CD and tape of "She Carries Me" have gone out into the world to offer succor in many situations. Jennifer receives letters and calls from people who have played it with dying friends and family members, who believe that it helped to ease the dying process. And people going through crises and losses in their lives have thanked her for her music. "People come up to me and tell me, you know, my mother who has cancer, or, my life was just totally falling apart and I listened to that . . . And someone told me she uses it to wake up to every day, she has it on her alarm radio."

This recalls to me those months in which I spent the first half-hour of each difficult day listening to "She

Carries Me," how it softened and strengthened me to go through the pain and loss that ruled my life at that time.

Jennifer and I try to come up with a way to describe this music; finally, wrinkling her forehead, she makes a try—"I guess you could call it a Kwan Yin pagan goddess mass." She smiles, lifting her hands, and then we laugh, understanding that the chant cuts across categories and belief systems to exist in its own unique resonance and strong evocation of Kwan Yin.

Four: Meditations, Practices, and Songs

How can you open the door so that Kwan Yin can enter your heart?

Asian devotees of Kwan Yin have been chanting to her and doing divination practices for centuries. Some contemporary women, thinking on Kwan Yin over the years, and holding her in our lives, have developed ways to contact her energy. Musicians and a meditation teacher have reached out to Kwan Yin with song. Other women do simple practices as reminders in their lives. One gave me her channeled communications from Kwan Yin and the Virgin Mary. And in my teaching, I have developed a guided meditation on Kwan Yin.

All these expressions I have gathered in this chapter. It begins with two simple practices; then shifts to the traditional chant, practices, and a song; and ends with a modern meditation, practices, and songs. May these approaches to Kwan Yin enliven your imagination and help you tap into her broad compassionate energy.

Making a Kwan Yin Altar

An altar is a device to help you focus your attention. It can be very simple—a shelf or other surface covered with a cloth and holding a picture or statue or other reminder of Kwan Yin. You may wish to add a candle and incense holder. A small vase of fresh flowers is always welcome. Sea shells, twigs, and other natural objects express our connection with the world of nature—the world of flowing water and trees and moon where Kwan Yin is so often pictured. Objects that you treasure will connect your altar strongly to you.

Your altar can be very simple or more ornate, as you express your own personality and esthetic sensibilities.

Place it somewhere in your living space where it will not be disturbed. When you want to meditate or contact Kwan Yin, you can sit down before your altar and find Kwan Yin's presence already there.

Begin the Day with Kwan Yin

Elaine Belle offers this suggestion:

Take some time each morning to meditate or sit quietly to compose yourself for your day. When you close your eyes, ask that Kwan Yin be with you. Ask that she fill your heart with compassion for yourself and others.

Traditional Chant

This is the recitation that I heard in the temples in China and that I chanted at City of Ten Thousand Buddhas. The words are: *"Namo Guan Shih Yin Pu-sa."*

Namo is an invocation, meaning "I call upon" or "I take refuge in." The Chinese character *Guan* means "look"; *Shih* means "world"; *Yin* means "sound." *Pusa* means "bodhisattva." The bodhisattva is the Buddhist meditator who delays her own full enlightenment to stay here in the world and save others.

So the chant can be loosely translated as:

"I call upon the bodhisattva who sees and hears the sufferings of the world."

This phrase, repeated over and over, has been used to venerate and invoke Kwan Yin for centuries. It has its own power. If you chant it to the traditional melody, for five minutes or more, you will find that the resonance of your voice and the intention to open to your deepest self may create an expanded state of consciousness.

Traditional Chant

A Divination Tool

There is a traditional form of divination derived from the "one hundred verses of Kwan Yin." These are ancient "poems" inspired by or based upon the bodhisattva of compassion. The verses address one hundred different basic human situations and point to the sacredness of nature and the immanence of the divine. In Chinese Buddhist temples they are consulted for guidance in one's life.

The book that fully explicates and presents these verses is called *Kuan Yin: Myths and Prophecies of the Chinese Goddess of Compassion,* by Palmer et al. This book is in print and readily available in paperback (see Books and Articles). While many of the verses may be obscure to the contemporary Western reader, they give a feeling for the rich world of Chinese culture from which Kwan Yin springs. For example:

#26 Illusion

Wild rumours run up and down among your colleagues,
From the blue edge of the horizon, guidance comes—
And what it seems to promise is *you shall be honoured*
But it doesn't stop you from tripping over on the ground.

#46 The Helper

The wise one's advice is: first of all, do nothing
Take care not to try anything at all ... stay still—
Wait for someone to come who can guide the work for you:
After times like this, the dying tree has flowered again.

Praise to Kwan Yin

This song was composed by Kuo-chou Rounds, a Buddhist meditator at the City of Ten Thousand Buddhas,

Gwan Yin Praise

and contains traditional wording, referring to lotus, moon, and willow. It can be found in the songbook *Songs of Awakening* (see Books and Articles).

Bowing to Kwan Yin

Kwan Yin can be part of the care of one's body, integrating the physical with the psychological and spiritual. Marylou Ledwell describes how she ends her daily session of yoga stretches.

"In the morning when I do my stretches, I finish the ones on the floor with the child pose, with my forehead touching the floor, at Kwan Yin's feet. In this posture of supplication, I will ask her to look out for friends and members of my support groups [Marylou has cancer] who are facing difficulties, as well as for myself."

Willow Willow

Several years ago, Carol Newhouse, a Buddhist teacher, heard that a dear friend had been diagnosed with breast cancer. Later she was sitting under a willow tree, struggling with her anger and sadness at this news. Through her tears of frustration, words came to her that seemed to be part of a song she remembered from childhood. (The song "Willow, Weep for Me" is a very familiar ballad.) She started softly singing her own words to the tune, as they came to her. "I remember feeling strange," Carol says, "because I am not really comfortable singing, especially when I feel upset. But I noticed as I sang to myself, my mind began to calm itself and I felt that all-encompassing compassion and presence that I have learned to call Kwan Yin. What emerged was a soft healing chant that I now use when I am feeling frustration and sadness.

Willow come to me. Willow come to me.
Bend your branches down along the ground and cover me.
Sad as I can be
Willow come to me.

Willow weep with me. Willow weep with me.
Bend your branches down and let your beauty cover me.
Come caress my skin, leaves so soft and thin
Willow weep with me.

Sad as I can be. Help me learn to see.
Willow weep with me.
Listen to my call. Help my tears to fall
Willow, willow weep with me.

(The original "Willow, Weep for Me"
was composed in 1932
by Ann Ronell.)

Guided Meditation on Kwan Yin

In my workshops I use a guided meditation that echoes the visions of women as disparate as an old Chinese nun and Hallie Iglehart, contemporary goddess chronicler. This Kwan Yin meditation can be done by the light of the full moon or simply by the light of your imagination. You may wish to record it so that you can play it and have the full experience of being guided.

Sit in a comfortable chair, close your eyes, let your body relax, and for a few moments pay attention to your breath.

Now, transport yourself to a beach on the ocean. Imagine your favorite stretch of sand next to water and place yourself there. It is a cloudy night. Hear the steady mutter of the waves, feel the warm sea breeze, smell the salt air.

Now look up to see a beautiful round full moon that has just risen.

Watch the moonlight shimmer on the water.

Gaze at the moon for a long time.

Now see it get brighter and brighter, until you can barely look at it.

Gradually, the moon becomes Kwan Yin herself, her body surrounded by a glowing aureole.

Slowly she descends toward you, until she stands on a lotus blossom that floats on the waves. She is a mature woman with Asian features, an ornate headdress, and flowing robe.

At sight of you, Kwan Yin smiles a beautiful smile, and tears of happiness shine in her eyes. She is so glad to see you.

As she comes closer, let her radiance enter you. Let her strength, her peace, and her compassion become a part of you. Let yourself open to her so that she merges completely with you.

In this moment, you feel bottomless compassion for yourself and all other creatures.

Your difficulties, your weaknesses, your inadequacies; all those ways in which you do not measure up to your own standards; all those moments in which you acted carelessly or unskillfully, or when you were immobilized by confusion; all your pain that sometimes seems endless, rising up when you least expect it—let these aspects of yourself be utterly accepted by you.

Feel your suffering and confusion surrounded by the love that Kwan Yin awakens in you. Let yourself surrender into her compassion for all life. And stay there as long as you need to.

Finally, it is time for Kwan Yin to leave. You see her in front of you again. As she moves away, she becomes smaller and smaller. At last the sea and sky vanish, too, and you rest in contemplation of the beautiful empty space that is left. Let yourself open into that space and experience it, so restful.

When you are ready, come back into this room, into your body, as you experience it sitting on the chair or pillow. Focus for a few moments, again, on your breath, until you are ready to open your eyes.

"Give Me a Hand, Kwan Yin"

This song was composed at City of Ten Thousand Buddhas by a *bhikshuni*, or nun, Heng-yin, whose sense of humor and musical gift greatly enlivened the community while she was there. It can be found in the songbook *Songs for Awakening* (see Books and Articles).

The Mount Shasta Communications: Texts to Meditate Upon

These are the channeled utterances collected by Gina Covina that come either from Kwan Yin alone or Kwan Yin and the Virgin Mary and others of the group of beings who spoke from Mount Shasta. They resonate

Give Me a Hand, Kuan Yin

with Kwan Yin's compassionate wisdom, and some recall obvious parallels to traditional associations; for example, the sea palm in its flexibility is like the traditional image of the willow tree that bends to the wind and springs up again.

When Gina gave me these fragments, I hung them up in my house, one next to the bathroom mirror, one on the kitchen cupboard, another where I could see it just before going out my door. As I have read them over and over, they have begun to permeate my consciousness. And sometimes I focus on one or another of them to contemplate in meditation.

I offer them here for your use. If any of these phrases awakens thoughts or feelings, please let them enrich and guide you.

> There is no more preparation—this *is* the transformation
>   for which you came.
> Every necessary condition is in place for every work there
>   is for you to do.
> Flow on through the days, easily, lightly, in love. We are
>   with you.

> Ask that your actions and thoughts
> bring the light of love into manifestation
> in the most powerful way given you.

> We are, you remember, the Mothers of this world.
> Surely we can nurture you.
> Let us lay our hands on your brow and lift the anxious
>   thoughts, when they gather.
> Let our rose light pour through your aura, loving every
>   particle and wave of you.

Wear our colors—
    blue and deep red for Mary's vibration,
    gold and rose and lavender for Kwan Yin—
        and green for the mountain.

Let our colors stream from your being.
Let the power gather.
We are with you for the transformation from dark to light
    of day.

Be as the sea palm—anchored to rock,
tossed by wind and heaving wave, returning upright
to bow again, never beaten, never uprooted,
always joyous in the bowing and in the springing upright.

The first impulse is the truest—
follow your heart the first time it whispers,
as wind does, through your being.

Let your open heart draw others open.
    Let the circle grow.
Let many hear these words and answer.
    Let the circle grow.

All places are sacred.
Water everywhere speaks our name.

Come openhearted, clear and filled with light.
We will meet you in our bodies of light.
You may see our forms on the mountain.

Come simply. Come in silence.
We will fill your beings with the Living Light, with the
    unfed flame,
with the everlasting touch of life.

Come singing. Come in love.
We will be there awaiting your arrival,
we will go with you every step of the way.

The calm river of your lives approaches the rocky chute of
    the rapids—flow on through.
You are the same water. The rocks cannot hurt you.
Remember, now and then, that you are the water and not
    the boat.
Flow on.

We are with you in peace and joy and in that rage that
    cleanses.
The violet transmuting flame is a flame. Fire cleanses.
Breathe your being through, now.

Heaven and the Underworld are aspects of the One path.
Both quests are necessary, channeling and journey, in light
    and darkness.
It is time to begin the new integration that will result in a
    commonly perceived spiritual reality,
a consensus of great power such as has not been felt on
    earth in many ages.

When you walk in the hills, you come closer to us
as the spirits of your animal protectors come closer to you.
Walk your animals—let us walk you.
We wait in our mountain for your springtime arrival.
We wait in your heart for your moment of listening.

"She Carries Me"

Jennifer Berezan's song puts the sublime emanation of
Kwan Yin in a country-western setting. "She carries

She Carries Me

1. She is a boat She is a light high on a
2. And though I walk through val-leys deep and sha-dows
3. A thou-sand arms a thou-sand eyes a thou-sand
4. She is the first She is the last She is the

hill in dark of night she is the way She is the
chase me in my sleep on roc-ky cliffs I stand a-
ears to hear my cries She is the gate She is the
fu - ture and the past Mo-ther of all of earth and

Last time to

deep She is the dark where an-gels sleep when all is
lone I have no name I have no home with bro-ken
dawn She leads me through and back once more when day is
sky She car-ries me to the oth-er side She car-ries

still and peace a-bides She car-ries me to the oth-er side
wings I reach to fly She car-ries me to the oth-er side
done and death is nigh She'll car-ry me to the oth-er side

Refrain

She car - ries me She car-ries me She car - ries

me to the oth - er side She car-ries me She car - ries

me She car-ries me to the oth - er side

me to the other side" is the heart of the song. "The other side," in Buddhist lore, indicates an altered state of consciousness, one of great equanimity and expansiveness, sometimes called enlightenment. In the song, "the other side" has other meanings as well—of comfort, peacefulness, death, and new life.

Jennifer's recording of this song is available from her at P.O. Box 3582, Oakland, CA 94609.

A Flower for the Goddess

Grace Harwood, a devotee of Kwan Yin, tells me she puts fresh flowers before her statue of the bodhisattva every day.

"It's the thing she likes best of all," Grace says with a smile so knowing that I believe Kwan Yin herself has spoken to her.

Books and Articles

BLOFELD, JOHN. *Bodhisattva of Compassion: The Mystical Tradition of Kuan Yin.* Boston: Shambhala Publications, 1977.

This is the classic study of Kwan Yin. Blofeld was a scholar of Buddhism who traveled and lived in Asia. The book is both a scholarly rumination on the mystical significance of Kwan Yin and an account of the author's encounters with her during his many years in China. It contains history, legends, lively anecdotes, descriptions of sacred rites, and translations of devotional poems and texts. A group of illustrations provides images of Kwan Yin.

CHING, JULIA. *Chinese Religions.* Maryknoll, NY: Orbis, 1993.

Among other topics, the author explores the role of women in Chinese antiquity. She assesses the influence of Buddhism and Taoism in Chinese society, describes the significance of the Queen Mother and other deities, and investigates the role of the shamaness and how that impacted society's view of the female.

DONEGAN, PAT, AND YOSHIE ISHIBASHI. *Chiyo-ni Woman Haiku Master.* Boston: Charles E. Tuttle, 1998.

Chiyo-ni is Japan's most famous woman haiku poet. Co-translator Donegan writes, "Besides being a haiku poet, Chiyo-ni was also a Buddhist nun in the Jodo-Shinshu sect. . . . I was immediately drawn to Chiyo-ni's haiku . . . to her vision and way of life, the fact that she actually *lived* the Way of Haiku—the practice of seeing the world clearly and compassionately, thereby appreciating each moment of one's everyday life."

LEE, PI-CHENG. *Kwan Yin's Saving Power.* Collected, translated, and edited by (Miss) Pi-Cheng Lee and published by her in England, 1932.

This curious little book offers "Some remarkable examples of response to appeal for aid, made to Kwan Yin by His devotees." [Note that Lee refers to Kwan Yin in the masculine.] Lee gathered stories from people cured of blindness and illness, saved from drowning and fire; people saved from captivity, from "bullets"; people who quickly recovered from injuries. The book ends with Lee's own story of her awakening of faith in Kwan Yin and subsequent veneration. She strongly emphasizes vegetarianism, which is typically associated with Kwan Yin devotion, and ends her story, "I am now a humanitarian, a vegetarian, and a Buddhist disciple."

PALMER, MARTIN, AND JAY RAMSAY, WITH MAN-HO KWOK. *Kuan Yin: Myths and Prophecies of the Chinese Goddess of Compassion.* London: Harper/Collins Publishers, Ltd., 1995.

A collaboration between a scholar, a poet, and a Chinese Buddhist master, this book delineates the history and

origins of Kwan Yin and then explores the myths and legends about her. But most intriguing is the section containing the one hundred poems associated with Kwan Yin,
which for centuries have been used for fortune-telling.
Each poem is printed on a separate page and illustrated
with a line drawing. The authors tell us how to use the
poems for divination.

REIS-HABITO, MARIA. "The Bodhisattva Guanyin
and the Virgin Mary." In *Buddhist-Christian Studies
13*. University of Hawaii Press, 1993.

The author explores the relationship between the Virgin
Mary and Kwan Yin, who is sometimes called "the Buddhist Madonna," in history and society. She notes that
both sacred female emanations are venerated for their
healing powers, both are worshiped particularly by
women, and both intercede on behalf of the dead as well
as the living. She compares the mystical dimensions of
Kwan Yin and Mary, speculating that they find a point of
convergence at the level of mysticism.

——. "The Great Compassion Dharani," *The Esoteric
Buddhist Tradition*. SBS Monographs no. 2 (1994).
Copenhagen and Aarhus.

"The Great Compassion Dharani of the Thousand-Armed
Avalokitesvara" (Kwan Yin) is a major text among Chinese,
Korean, and Japanese Buddhists. Reis-Habito describes its
origin and history, and how it has been used down through
the ages.

——. "The Repentance Ritual of the Thousand-Armed
Guanyin." *Studies in Central and East Asian Religions*, vol. 4 (autumn 1991).

The author looks at three aspects of this important ritual:
1. its source and historical development,
2. the meaning of "repentance" in this sacred context, and
3. the ritual's "backdrop of Confucian ancestor worship, filial piety, and the Buddhist belief in transmigration."

SCHUSTER, NANCY. "Striking a Balance: Women and Images of Women in Early Chinese Buddhism." In *Women, Religion, and Social Change,* ed. Yvonne Yazbeck Haddad and Ellison-Banks Findly. Albany, NY: State University of New York Press, 1985.

This article explores the treatment of women in Buddhist scriptures and concentrates on women in Chinese Buddhism, exploring women's options in early Medieval China. The author presents the history and legacy of Chinese Buddhist nuns.

Songs for Awakening. San Francisco Sino-American Buddhist Association, 1979. Available from Gold Mountain Monastery, 1731–15th St., San Francisco, CA 94103.

This eighty-eight-page songbook contains songs composed by students of the Chinese Venerable Master Hua at City of Ten Thousand Buddhas. They range from devotional songs with traditional texts to the ironically playful verses of the nun Heng-yin. (Heng-yin made a recording called "Awakening" of some of these songs set to original country-western and rock tunes.) This attractive songbook is illustrated with line drawings, calligraphy, and photographs of nature and of the nuns and other students at City of Ten Thousand Buddhas.

STEIN, DIANE. *A Woman's I Ching.* Freedom, CA: The Crossing Press, 1997.

The *I Ching* is one of the oldest written documents in the world, dating from the prepatriarchal world of ancient China. Here is a feminist interpretation of this method for divining the future. Stein has removed sexist language and imagery, reclaiming the feminine content of the original work and creating a woman's tool for finding our way in our lives.

The Essential Reiki Journal, P.O. Box 1436, Olney, MD 20830–1436.

This periodical offers articles on the healing art of Reiki, flower and gemstone essences, and other topics, as well as ads for sacred objects and books by Diane Stein. The editor, Robyn Zimmerman, writes, "This Journal is published in cooperation with Diane Stein, a major contributing writer and the creator of the Essential Essences mother tinctures. Our goal is to provide Diane's many students, as well as other interested Reiki Practitioners, with an ongoing source of information, ideas, and products, as they take their gift of healing into the world."

THYNN THYNN, Dr. *Living Meditation, Living Insight*. Available from Sae Taw Win Dhamma Center, 7415 Hayden Ave., Sebastopol, CA 95472. Telephone: (707) 829-9857.

A book of questions and answers about the Dharma, Dharma teacher Dr. Thynn Thynn speaks about meditation in action, the Four Noble Truths in daily life, mindfulness and awareness, creative living, and many other topics. Down-to-earth advice on how to integrate spiritual prac- tice into the moments of our mundane existences.

VON KOERBER, HANS NORDEWIN. "Kuan Yin, the Buddhist Madonna." *The Theosophical Forum* (July 1941).

An exploration of the "madonna-concept," as the author calls it, as it developed in Asia, particularly through the figure of Kwan Yin. The article contains historical information and interesting reflections on the importance of certain materials being used to fashion Kwan Yin statues: for example, the qualities expressed by sandalwood or jade, ivory or rock-crystal, clay or porcelain.

YU, ANTHONY C., ED. *The Journey to the West.* Four volumes. Chicago: University of Chicago Press, 1977–1983.

This popular Chinese novel was written in the 1570s by Wu-Cheng. In one hundred chapters, it chronicles the journey of the monk Hsuan Tsang (who lived in the seventh century) to India to find and bring back Buddhist scriptures. While Hsuan Tsang was an actual historical figure, Wu-Cheng added the imaginary characters of the Monkey King, Great Sage Equal to Heaven, Pigsy, Sandy, and others to enliven the pilgrim's adventures. Kwan Yin appears now and then in the book to give advice or bring salvation to one of the characters. You can find her in chapters 6, 8, 12, 17, 26, 42, 49, and 71.

YÜ, CHÜN-FANG. "A Sutra Promoting the White-Robed Guanyin as Giver of Sons." In *Religions of China in Practice,* ed. Donald S. Lopez, Jr. Princeton, NJ: Princeton University Press, 1996, pp. 97–105.

Yü explores the history of the White-Robed Kwan Yin through scriptures and other documents, giving examples of the miraculous births of sons attributed to the bodhisattva.

——. "Feminine Images of Kuan-yin in Post-T'ang China." *Journal of Chinese Religions,* no. 18 (fall 1990).

This major article describes the bodhisattva's transformation from the male Avalokitesvara to the female Kwan Yin.
The author then gives the scholarly sources for, and tells
the stories of the various forms of, Kwan Yin in China, such
as Princess Miao-Shan, the Kwan Yin of the South Sea,
Kwan Yin with Fish Basket, and so forth. Very full descriptions, with copious footnotes.

——. "Guanyin: The Chinese Transformation of Ava-
lokiteshvara." In *Latter Days of the Law: Images of
Chinese Buddhism 850–1850*, ed. Marsha Weidner.
Spence Museum of Art, University of Kansas in association with University of Hawaii Press, 1994.

Another description of the transformation of the bodhisattva from male to female. In this article Yü looks at the
"water and moon" Kwan Yin and gives its significance. She
recounts stories of some other Kwan Yin manifestations
and tells how their development was helped along by mira-
cles and pilgrimage traditions, popularized by art and literature; and she suggests that each distinct Kwan Yin was
anchored in one specific place. A rich evocation.

——. "Not Merely Patriarchy: Matriarchal Bodhisattvas
and Female Masters in Chinese Buddhism." Paper
given at Conference on Professor Rita Gross's *Buddhism After Patriarchy*, April 20–22, 1995, at Trinity
College of Toronto.

This is a general introduction to Kwan Yin in China. The
author then describes a contemporary woman master in
Taiwan, named Cheng-yen. This living Kwan Yin heads a
grass-roots organization, the Merit Association of Compassion Relief, which has established Buddhist hospitals and
offers aid to the needy. Cheng-yen's organization now

includes more than 3.5 million members, and her chapters exist in at least eleven countries. In the eyes of the members of the Merit Association, "Cheng-yen is Kwan-yin made flesh."

——. "P'u-t'o Shan: Pilgrimage and the Creation of the Chinese Potalaka." In *Pilgrims and Sacred Sites in China*, ed. Susan Naquin and Chün-fang Yü. Berkeley: University of California Press, 1992.

A description of P'u-T'o Shan, or Pu To Island, the island in the South China Sea, off Shanghai, where Kwan Yin is said to reside. Yü explores the creation of this sacred site and its history as a place of pilgrimage for the Chinese people.

Credits

Two haiku excerpted from *Chiyo-ni Woman Haiku Master* by Pat Donegan and Yoshie Ishibushi, © 1998. Published by Charles E. Tuttle Company, Inc., Rutland, Vermont, and Tokyo, Japan. Permission given by Charles E. Tuttle Company.

Verses #26 and #46 from *Kuan Yin: Myths and Revelations of the Chinese Goddess of Compassion,* by Martin Palmer and Jay Ramsay with Man-Ho Kwok. Published by HarperCollins Publishers Ltd., London, 1995. Permission given by HarperCollins Ltd.

"She Carries Me," song composed and performed by Jennifer Berezan. Permission of the composer.

"Goddess Give Us Strength to Cut Through," silk screen by Mayumi Oda. Permission of the artist.

"Guan Yin Praise" by Kuo-chou Rounds and "Give Me a Hand, Kuan Yin" by Heng-yin, two songs, as reproduced in *Songs for Awakening.* Published by San Francisco: Sino-American Buddhist Association, 1979. Permission of Sino-American Buddhist Association.

Acknowledgments

The writing of a book can be a somewhat mysterious process, a bit like cooking, as you reach here and there for ingredients, gratefully receive what comes from the universe, mix it all together, slide it into the oven, and hope for the best.

If there were recipes to follow, they came in large part from the pre-eminent scholar of Kwan Yin in America, Dr. Chün-fang Yü, whose many articles on the bodhisattva have informed and delighted me and greatly enlarged my understanding. I thank Dr. Yü for her meticulous scholarship and keen insight into the history and significance of Kwan Yin in China. The works of other scholars and poets, such as John Blofeld, Martin Palmer, Jay Ramsay, and Maria Reis-Habito, have been of great help in preparing this book.

The ingredients for this meal came from many directions. Phyllis Pay journeyed with me to China to greet Kwan Yin on her own soil; your perspective, Phyllis, balanced and deepened my own. Mary Watkins, a spiritually gifted musician and composer, wrote, performed, and recorded the music that comforted me in rough moments, as well as notating two of the songs in Chapter Four. Thanks to Judy Clarence for her help with library research and to Kathryn Poethig for giving me access to the UC Berkeley Library collection. I thank the graphic artists whose work I have reproduced in this book, many of them anonymous even though I made great efforts to find them, for their unique, beautiful evocations of the goddess herself. Mayumi Oda particularly enriches my understanding of Kwan Yin with her many surprising interpretations.

My gratitude goes to my friends Nan Gefen and Marcia Freedman for their very useful comments on an early draft of this book. Tisha Hooks, my editor at Beacon Press, gave support and helpful advice as the book progressed.

A major ingredient of any concoction associated with Kwan Yin must be compassion. During the writing of the book, I was instructed in this quality by a number of people, whether they knew it or not. Among them, Crystal Juelson (who did know it) and Grace Harwood, and my late brother-in-law Lewis Clipp. There is no escaping life's lessons, and to even contemplate the goal of a compassionate response to them is to set oneself an arduous task. Kwan Yin watched over my efforts, no doubt chuckling and weeping by turns.

On the home front, my landlords Suzanne Savage and Lew Carson, along with my cat George and their cat Mo and numerous backyard birds and squirrels, contributed to the serenity necessary to accomplish the task of writing this book. And the Redwood Regional Park System on the ridge above Oakland provided woodland trails on which I could hike undisturbed and open myself to Kwan Yin's presence.

Finally, Kwan Yin herself stood at my elbow as I gathered and chopped, stirred and cooked. I invited her spirit into my place, spoke to her at difficult times, petitioned her often to give me a hand. Thank you, Kwan Yin, for hearing my cries and helping me to step more fully into the moment-by-moment reality of my experience. May this book bring your presence and voice into the lives of many.